in your ministry


Alan and Karen Sell

# One Ministry,
## *Many Ministers*

# One Ministry, *Many Ministers*

A Case Study from the Reformed Tradition

ALAN P. F. SELL

PICKWICK *Publications* · Eugene, Oregon

ONE MINISTRY, MANY MINISTERS
A Case Study from the Reformed Tradition

Copyright © 2014 Alan P. F. Sell. All rights reserved. Except for brief quotations in critical publications or reviews, no part of this book may be reproduced in any manner without prior written permission from the publisher. Write: Permissions, Wipf and Stock Publishers, 199 W. 8th Ave., Suite 3, Eugene, OR 97401.

Pickwick Publications
An Imprint of Wipf and Stock Publishers
199 W. 8th Ave., Suite 3
Eugene, OR 97401

www.wipfandstock.com

ISBN 13: 978-1-62564-892-1

*Cataloguing-in-Publication data:*

Sell, Alan P. F..

One ministry, many ministers : a case study from the Reformed tradition / Alan P. F. Sell.

xii + 134 pp. ; 23 cm. Includes bibliographical references and indices.

ISBN 13: 978-1-62564-892-1

1. Pastoral theology—Reformed Church. 2. Reformed Church—Clergy. 3. Dissenters—Religious—Great Britain—History. 4. Ministry and Christian union. I. Title.

BV4012 S45 2014

Manufactured in the U.S.A.

To

Hugh Kember, exemplary minister of the gospel,
who delivered the charge to the minister at my ordination,

and

Clyde Binfield,
friend, scholar, and "layman"
who knows more than most about ministry

Jesus calls us! By thy mercies,
Saviour, may we hear thy call,
Give our hearts to thy obedience,
Serve and love thee best of all.

CECIL FRANCES ALEXANDER (1818–95)

# Contents

# Preface

THIS BOOK CONCERNS THE nature of Christian ministry and the work and education of ministers. It takes the form of a case study of this important theme as it was understood in the predecessor traditions of The United Reformed Church, which have in turn informed that church's current practice. I hope that what I have done will at least interest the ministers of the gospel and the visible saints (that is, the church members) of The United Reformed Church as they reflect upon their several ministries. I should also like to think that it may be of help to those of other Christian traditions who work alongside United Reformed ministers and people in ecumenical pastorates. The experience of international ecumenical work in which I have been privileged to share prompts me to think that my findings are relevant not only to the wider Reformed communion, but that they may even make a modest contribution to inter-communion discussions of ministry. Were they to do so, I should be delighted.

The United Reformed Church was constituted in 1972 by the union of the Congregational Church in England and Wales with the Presbyterian Church of England. Subsequently, in 1981, the Re-formed Association of Churches of Christ (ecclesiastical relatives of the American Christian Church [Disciples of Christ]) came into the union, and in 2000 the majority of the churches of the Congregational Union of Scotland did likewise. The United Reformed Church is a member of the World Communion of Reformed Churches and of the World Council of Churches.

Although, being less than fifty years old, The United Reformed Church is relatively young, its roots reach back to the English Reformation of the sixteenth century when, on doctrinal grounds, the Separatist harbingers of Congregationalism proposed, suffered, and even died for, an understanding of the church contrary to that espoused by the Church of

England. From that time onwards ministry has been offered within the ensuing traditions by thousands of people in numerous places and in a variety of ways. In this book I am concerned with the current context in which United Reformed Christians—whether ministers of the gospel or not—are called upon to exercise their gifts. Not, indeed, that this is one more "how to do ministry today" book, necessary and helpful though such books may be. Rather, I seek to illuminate our understanding of what ministry is, and who the ministers are, by reference both to the Bible and to our heritage. We stand in the apostolic succession of those who have proclaimed the gospel of Christ, and I believe that we miss a great deal if we do not learn and derive encouragement from those in whose steps we follow.

The United Reformed Church holds in trust a number of principles that have flowed down to us from our forebears in the faith. The ways in which we have been called upon to practise them have varied in accordance with changing socio-political times and circumstances, but I believe that the principles stand. Among them is the conviction that the one church catholic comprises all, on earth and in heaven, who, on the ground of Christ's saving work, have been granted new life, called and gathered together by God the Holy Spirit, and engrafted as branches into Christ the Vine. Since all thus called cannot be other than united to one another because they are one in Christ, all of them are in principle welcome at the Lord's table in our church; after all, it is not ours, but *his*.

Again, we believe that Jesus Christ is the only Lord of the church (hence our Nonconformity where church establishment is concerned); and in our conciliar structure of Church Meeting, Synod, and General Assembly, we honour our conviction that God the Holy Spirit addresses his people whenever they gather to seek his will for their life and mission. Our church order thus demands mutual oversight as between these *foci* of churchly life, and offers ample scope for the witness and service of all the members. I believe that we do well if we live by these principles (which, being sinners as well as saints, we have not always done), witness to them in ecumenical contexts, and pass them on to those who come after us.

I trust that it will become clear that I have a high view of Christian ministry—both that of every Christian, and that of ministers of the gospel. To serve, however imperfectly, under the one ministry of Christ is a high calling and a great privilege. As for ministers of the gospel, I am only too conscious of the multifarious tasks they are called upon undertake at the present time. I continue to believe, however, that the conduct of worship, the preaching of the gospel through word and sacramental action, and the pastoral care and Christian education of the people remain of vital importance, not least if the varied ministries of all the members are to be well-grounded and encouraged. Accordingly, I have focused upon these four tasks.

I should like to explain, first, that while, when speaking or writing of males and females together, I believe it right to use inclusive language, our forebears, according to the convention of their times, used such words as "man" and "mankind" as all-embracing terms. Since everybody understands this, I have not altered their quoted language, believing that we can without difficulty "hear" what they wrote in the way they intended it. It is, however, regrettable that some modern writers, long after the ordination of Constance Coltman in 1917, were still writing as if our ministers of the gospel were exclusively male. Secondly, in order to avoid cluttering the text with bracketed dates and explanatory sentences, I have supplied a Descriptive Index of Persons.

This book is better than it would otherwise have been had I not submitted it to the learned, experienced, and rigorous scrutiny of the Revd Dr David Cornick and the Revd Dr David Peel. I am most grateful for their comments. I have sought to agree with them wherever I can (albeit they did not always agree with each other), and I hope that they will be able to feel that, at least at certain points, I listened and took appropriate action. I should also like to thank the Revd Dr Robert Pope for his continuing encouragement of my work; and my wife, Dr Karen Sell, for the invaluable contribution she has made to our (I use the word advisedly) ministry over more than five decades.

Finally, I am most grateful to Dr. K. C. Hanson, Editor-in-chief, and Dr. Robin Parry, this book's editor, for their continuing confidence in my work; and to all colleagues at Wipf & Stock for their courtesy and helpfulness, and for the high standards which they unfailingly attain.

**Alan P. F. Sell**
University of Wales Trinity Saint David
University of Chester

# 1

# Introduction

LIKE WILLIAM JAY OF Argyle Congregational Church, Bath, I was a boy preacher: we both delivered our first public sermon at the age of sixteen. Unlike William Jay, I did not subsequently remain in one pastorate for sixty-two years. On the contrary, I left regular pastoral charge forty-five years ago. In the eyes of some this may suffice to disqualify me for writing on the ministry, for in many respects church life has undergone a sea-change since 1968. In fact, however, I, who regard myself as a creature of the villages who envisaged a life-time in rural pastorates, have had the quite unexpected privilege of ministering in a variety of ways in many parts of the world. I have had opportunities of teaching students, some of them destined for ministry, in both church and secular institutions at home and abroad. I have learned much from discussing the nature and content of ministerial education with those responsible for providing it in five continents, and I have participated in numerous ecumenical discussions of ministry and other neuralgic topics.

In what follows I set out from the conviction that the primary ministry is that of the risen and ascended Christ, the one Lord of the church, and that he deigns to exercise it not only through those who are called to be ministers of the gospel, but through all the saints. For they, no less than the ministers, are called to use the gifts they have received in witness and service within and beyond the church. In attempting to make this case, I shall draw upon my experience as appropriate, but, much more importantly, I shall seek to recall my readers to the biblically-rooted heritage of reflection on the ministry to which we of The United Reformed Church are heirs. We shall find that over the past 450 years it has been consistently held by our predecessor traditions and ourselves that ministers of the gospel are to lead the church's worship, to preach the gospel and give pastoral care, and to educate the saints in the faith so that they may the more effectively perform their several ministries. We shall also find that as regards the preparation of our ministers of the gospel, it has never been the case that "one size fits all." People have come into the ministry by a variety of routes, and they have been educated through courses which have been diverse in location, content, and academic level. But all of our ministers have stood, or stand, in the noble succession of those who have proclaimed the apostles' gospel through the Christian ages, and many of them have much to teach us. Accordingly, as well as pondering our present situation, we shall "Remember the days of old" (Deut 32: 7). We shall do this not in the interests of nostalgia, or of escaping from current challenges, but because we recognise that we are not the first to have undertaken, or reflected upon, ministry. But let our remembering be of the Hebrew sort.

According to the ancient narrative, when Moses' successor, Joshua, had successfully led the wandering Hebrews over the river Jordan into the promised land of Canaan, he ordered one man from each of the twelve tribes of Israel to gather one stone, and for these to be erected as a memorial. Then Joshua said, "In days to come, when your children ask what these stones mean, you will tell them how the waters of the Jordan were cut off before the Ark of the Covenant of the Lord. . . . These stones will always be a reminder to the Israelites" (Josh 4: 6–7). In other words, uninscribed mounds of stone require interpretation, and as the years pass by memory is required, and the memory must be handed on from generation to generation. Why? Not simply so that as a matter of interest later generations shall know what happened in the past, but so that they will give thanks to the God who did great things, reconsecrate themselves to his service, mend their ways, and go forward in obedience and faith. Hebrew remembering is a matter of recalling the past into the present so that it revitalizes us for the future. It is to recall the past in such a way that we do not stagnate, but go forward strengthened by it. Is not this exactly what we do as often as we gather at the Lord's table? Through words and actions we recall who Jesus is and what he has done for us in the victory of the Cross, and we go forward thankfully, strengthened and rejoicing in his continuing presence, eager to proclaim and live by the good news of his love. Our remembering can only be done, and our reinvigorated witness can only be made, in the context in which we have been set.

With these preliminary thoughts in mind, we turn now to consider the nature and work of ministry, and the education of the ministers.

# 2

# The Nature of Ministry

## THE MINISTRY OF CHRIST AND OF ALL THE SAINTS

WHEN WE READ OR hear about "the ministry," I suppose that our thoughts tend to fly to those whom we call "the minister." Or we may think, like Paul, of the diversities of ministries that are to be found in the church. We need to remember that all of the forms of ministry with which we are familiar need to be seen in the light of the fact that there is really one ministry only in the church, namely, that of the risen Christ himself. Nobody put it more crisply than T. W. Manson: "There is only one 'essential ministry' in the Church, the perpetual ministry of the Risen and Ever-Present Lord Himself."[1] A document of the Presbyterian Church of Canada helpfully fills out this statement:

> There is only one ministry of redemption for the world, that of Jesus Christ. He is the living Word of God, the source and steward of all power and authority for ministry. All ministries of the Church proceed from and are sustained by the ministry of the Lord Jesus Christ. When patterned on the example of Christ, the diverse ministries of the Church will be grounded in the creative and redemptive purposes of God, exercised through the presence of Christ, and sustained by the power of the Holy Spirit.[2]

1. Manson, *The Church's Ministry*, 100.

2. Anon., "Towards a Framework of a Theology and Practice of Ministry in the

To this T. F. Torrance adds the important truth that to follow the example of Christ is to participate "in the obedience of Christ."[3]

Although the church is called to model Christ's ministry in its own life, and to be about Christ's business in the world, I think that we seriously overstate our position as the people of God if we say, as some do, that the church is a prolongation, continuation, or extension of the incarnation of Christ. Such language unduly exalts the church and unintentionally diminishes the significance of *the* incarnation. P. T. Forsyth's curt rebuttal of the notion may stand: "that which owes itself to a rebirth cannot be the prolongation of the ever sinless."[4] The church comprises believers, saints, who have made a Spirit-enabled response to the call of God's grace in the gospel. But, as the slightest glance at some of the New Testament epistles would confirm—indeed, significant tracts of the epistles would not have been written had the saints been behaving themselves—the saints remain sinners on the path of sanctification. By grace we become Christians, not Christs—even little ones; and this applies both to the individual Christian and to the church at large.

The wonder is that despite his treasure being in an earthen vessel, Christ's continuing ministry is performed through the *laos* (laity), the people of God, and every member is called to offer such gifts as have been received in service to, and through, the whole company: "There is a ministry to be fulfilled by the whole Church, through all its individual members and through its corporate life."[5] Some forms of ministry are general in nature: we are all called to witness for Christ, to uphold one another in prayer, and to bear one another's burdens. Other ministries are more specific: they are particular callings addressed by God to those relevantly gifted. The New Testament records a number of these, including apostles, prophets, evangelists, pastors, and teachers (Eph 4:11–12); and let us not forget the callings of such as Ephraim Tellwright. He was a Methodist local preacher, but "It was in the finance of salvation that he rose supreme—the interminable alteration of debt-raising and new liability which provides a lasting excitement for Nonconformists. . . . The minister by his leading might bring sinners to the penitent form, but it was Ephraim Tellwright who reduced the

---

Presbyterian Church of Canada," 3.

3. Torrance, *Conflict and Agreement in the Church*, II, 16.

4. Forsyth, *The Church and the Sacraments*, 83.

5. *A Declaration of Faith* (The Congregational Church in England and Wales, 1967), in Thompson, *Stating the Gospel*, 230.

cost per head of souls saved, and so widened the frontiers of the Kingdom of Heaven."[6] The purpose of the particular ministries within the church is to enable all the saints to fulfil their vocations as servants and witnesses for Christ, not only within the church, but out in the world.

What great service has been rendered by the faithful testimony of the saints! Referring to the early Christian centuries, T. W. Manson observed that

> The great preachers came after Constantine the Great; and before that Christianity had already done its work and made its way right through the Empire from end to end. When we try to picture how it was done we seem to see domestic servants teaching Christ in and through their domestic service, workers doing it through their work, small shopkeepers through their trade, and so on, rather than eloquent propagandists swaying mass meetings of interested enquirers. It is still true that the best propaganda for genuine Christianity is genuine Christians.[7]

It is sobering for ministers of the gospel to ponder the fact that some impressive advances of the Christian mission occurred when they were nowhere to be seen. During the English Civil War, for example, a number of ministers fled for safety from Wales to London, among them Walter Cradock of Llanvaches. In a sermon he wrote,

> I have observed, and seen, in the Mountains of Wales . . . the Gospel is run over the Mountaines between Brecknockshire and Monmouthshire, as the fire in the thatch; and who should doe this? They have no Ministers: but some of the wisest say, there are about 800 godly people, and they goe from one to another. They have no Ministers, it is true; if they had, they would honour them and blesse God for them: and shall we raile at such, and say they are Tubpreachers, and they were never at the University? Let us fall downe, and honour God. . . . They were filled with good newes, and they tell it to others.[8]

The ministry, under Christ, of the whole people of God is sometimes referred to as the priesthood of all believers. This phrase has been

---

6. Bennett, *Anna of the Five Towns*, 32. This author of fiction knew of what he wrote.

7. Manson, *Ministry and Priesthood: Christ's and Ours*, 21. We might also note that among other aspects of the early Christian witness were care for the poor and needy and fearlessness in face of death.

8. Cradock, *Glad Tydings from Heaven*, 50.

understood to mean that every believer has direct access to God through Jesus Christ the one Mediator, without the mediation of a priest; and this is undoubtedly the case (1 Tim 2: 5). Sadly, however, the thought can become warped into that unfortunate individualism which suggests that in the church every individual's opinion is as good as that of anyone else, and that all the offices of the church are open to all (which repudiates the idea of particular callings in relation to gifts bestowed). But I think that the primary meaning of the phrase is corporate: we are invited to think of the priesthood of all the people together (1 Pet 2: 9). A priesthood is a corporate entity, and this becomes important, for example, when we are thinking about the Lord's Supper. For it is the church, the corporate priesthood of believers, which keeps the Supper; the sacrament is not "done to" the saints by members of a priestly caste. In a discussion paper, a committee of The United Reformed Church was concise to the point of bluntness on this matter. In response to the statement in the *Final Report* of the Anglican-Roman Catholic International Commission that the ministry of priests "is not an extension of the common Christian priesthood, but belongs to another realm of the gifts of the Spirit," our people retorted, "We do not recognise another realm."[9] At the Lord's Supper the members of the priesthood of believers, individually and together and in the presence of the risen Lord, offer themselves for sacrificial service after the pattern of Christ, and they do this "till he come"; and Christ, our great high priest, gathers the offering of his whole church and presents it to the Father.

With the strong emphasis upon the ministry of the laity which we find in the literature of the World Council of Churches—especially in the report presented at the Faith and Order conference held at Montreal in 1963, there has grown up the notion that all church members receive their ordination to ministry at their baptism. This, I think, is not a helpful approach, notwithstanding the fact that Martin Luther called baptism the "sacrament of ordination." In the first place, reference is frequently made to the baptism of Jesus by John the Baptist, whose baptism was one of repentance and the forgiveness of sins, which Jesus did not need. Secondly, therefore, his baptism is often construed as the occasion on which Jesus was commissioned to embark upon his ministry. If this be accepted, one can see an analogy with believer baptism, where a person professes faith and enters upon the life

---

9. *Patterns of Ministry in The United Reformed Church*, a paper prepared for discussion and action at the General Assembly of 1992, 3. The authors quote the ARCIC *Final Report*, 36.

of discipleship within the fellowship of the church. Believer baptism of the previously unbaptized had always been a possibility within the Congregational and Presbyterian traditions which flowed into The United Reformed Church—and this not only on the mission field; and it was from the outset the practice of the Churches of Christ, and was a significant aspect of the contribution which, in 1981, they brought into the union. However, it is harder to think of infant baptism as the commissioning of a person to a lifetime of ministry, for a personal response to a call from God is not, and cannot be, present; yet such a response is integral to a person's ordination. Above all else, the sacrament of infant baptism witnesses to the gospel truth that God's grace goes before us, and that before we can do anything, God does everything. Baptized children of the covenant are members of the church, but as catechumens. Infant baptism marks the beginning of a process of learning and nurture which will, it is hoped, lead in due time to profession of faith and personal acceptance of responsibilities within the ministry and mission of the church. This, is why, for example, when a pastorate is vacant we tend not to involve infants named on the cradle roll in the calling of ministers; but following a person's profession of faith at years of discretion, such involvement is rightly expected.

Although we of The United Reformed Church feel a little uneasy about the term "layperson" when used as if the ministers of the gospel were separated out from the people of God,[10] the fact remains that of all the traditions within the church, we have made it at least as possible as any other denomination for our "layfolk" actually to offer their several ministries. We have not simply mouthed words concerning "the ministry of the whole people of God," we have provided for its exercise in our polity. In particular, in our local churches every professed saint is a member of the Church Meeting, about which I shall have more to say in the following chapter; and by the Church Meeting some members are called into the eldership. Elders are ordained for life, and they serve for locally specified terms. The minister normally presides at their meetings and they, together with the minister, have among their responsibilities, those of ensuring that worship takes place in due order, that pastoral care is given, and that constructive relations are maintained with the wider councils of the Church.

---

10. See further, John, *Congregationalism in an Ecumenical Era.*

## THE MINISTERS OF THE GOSPEL

Where, in all of this, are those who are widely known as ministers of Word and Sacrament (though I prefer to call them ministers of the gospel, because God the Holy Spirit calls and gathers the church as people are enabled to respond to the good news of God's saving grace, and to this the Bible and the sacraments bear witness)? We have already seen that they are of the *laos*, the people of God, and that every member is called to a more or less specialized form of ministry. This means, to repeat, that while ministers do not belong to a special priestly caste, we cannot say that every member is entitled to perform the functions of leading worship, publicly proclaiming the gospel, serving at the Lord's table and font, and offering pastoral care; for what ministers of the gospel do turns upon the specific call they have received. Their God-given gifts have been discerned in them by the churchly fellowship, and the church (both locally and more widely) receives their gifts and commissions them in the conviction that, as far as may be known, God has called and ordained them for his service.[11]

Traditionally, in many of our services of ordination, the ordinands testified to their religious experience, stated their faith, and explained the steps whereby the Lord had brought them to this ministry. The eminent and urbane nineteenth-century Congregational minister, John Stoughton, recalled that the churches "were all very particular in requiring from the candidate a statement of Christian experience, a distinct confession of Christian belief, and a clear expression of ecclesiastical principles."[12] I find it sad that in our current and recent service books this practice has become optional, and that some ordinands are content to answer printed questions concerning belief and practice that are formally put to them.

---

11. The Term "ordination" came relatively late into the Congregational vocabulary: "recognition" was widely used. "Ordination" was traditionally viewed with suspicion because of its association in some Christian traditions with the doctrine that at ordination the candidate is placed within a special order, and undergoes an ontological change as sacramental power (*potestas*) is bestowed which is not available to those outside of the priestly order. The term is studiously avoided in "The [Savoy] Institution of Churches and the Order Appointed in them by Jesus Christ" 1658, and in *A Declaration of Faith* 1967. For these documents see Thompson, ed., *Stating the Faith*. However, the widely used *Manual for Ministers*, first published in 1936, included a service for "The Ordination of a Minister." By contrast, the term "ordination" (without any untoward sacerdotal connotations) was, historically, current in the Presbyterian tradition. See, for example, *The Directory for the Publick Worship of God*, 1645.

12. Stoughton, *Reminiscences of Congregationalism*, 21.

Again, at ordination we pray that ministers will be equipped by God for their awesome task but, once more, we do not think that they become different in kind or status from any other member. Certainly they are to stand for Christ before the people. That is to say, they are not simply called to perform certain functions, though as Robert Paul rightly reminds us, the ministry "is concerned with function. We must resist the kind of theological snobbery that refuses to see any relationship between Ministerial orders and the practical tasks of building up the Church for worship and witness."[13] The ministers are set apart for specific tasks. But more than that, they are to be people in whom others can see the Lord who has called, equipped and commissioned them. They pursue their calling among the saints, not from some Olympian height above them; they stand before the saints in the name of Christ, and they encourage the saints to stand before the world in that same name. This the saints will do as they offer their gifts and make their witness in the circles in which they move. The authority possessed by ministers of the gospel is not bestowed upon them by the church at ordination or at any other time, "else the message of the Word would be no message to the Church, but only its soliloquy";[14] least of all is it obtained by their own efforts. It comes from Christ the head of the church as a gift to the church.[15] At an ordination service the church acknowledges the source of the gift, receives the gift, and vows to fulfil its responsibilities towards the newly ordained minister. Christ remains the great shepherd of his flock; the ministers remain under-shepherds—a high calling indeed, and one implying accountability and obedience to the Lord of the church.

## REFLECTIONS ON THE CALL TO THE GOSPEL MINISTRY

While there is much to be said for encouraging those with sincere convictions and appropriate gifts to consider the gospel ministry, nobody can sense a call for anyone else. Among the many tales that flow down in the folk memory of our tradition is that of the mother who assured Newman Hall that her son had the makings of an apostle, even though his talent was buried in a napkin. Under pressure, Hall agreed to interview the son. Afterwards he replied to the mother thus: "Dear Madam, I have shaken the

13. Paul, *Ministry*, 116.

14. Forsyth, *The Church and the Sacraments*, 138.

15. See Calvin, *Commentary on Ephesians* 4:11.

napkin, but there is no talent."[16] It is well that assessment committees proceed responsibly and diligently lest they refuse one called by God. It is recorded that Edward Moore, who was subsequently ordained and exercised an energetic ministry, was initially refused extra-mural ministerial training "on the somewhat curious grounds that he had one leg shorter than the other." On his own behalf the reporter, Principal E. S. Kiek of Parkin College, Adelaide, drily adds, "the experience of the present writer is that such refusals are generally due rather to deficiency at the other end."[17] David Peel addresses a cautionary word to members of assessment committees when he writes, "In our person-centred culture we are sometimes not brave enough to weigh the balance of doubt in favour of the church rather than the candidate."[18]

It is for the good of both those who sense a call to the gospel ministry and the church that their call is graciously and probingly tested. It is, for example, possible for a person to have an inflated appreciation of his or her gifts; to have a psychological *need* of the problems of others; to have an authoritarian attitude which is the obverse of "meek and lowly in heart." It is more than likely that any such persons who did find their way into the ministry would be most unhappy, and, in all probability, so would their churches. For this reason candidates for ministry are often brought together at conferences with a view both to acquainting them with the nature and challenges of the ministry, and to seeing how they relate to others. In some instances methods of psychological testing are used.

Over and above such personality issues, there is the question, Why does this enquirer wish to be a minister? On a number of occasions, when I have asked that question, the response has been, "Because I want to help people." I then gently suggest that medical doctors, teachers, social workers and many others help people. I repeat my question, Why do you wish to be a minister? Silence reigns. Does the person not value the high privilege of leading worship, I wonder? Has he or she no gospel to proclaim? Almost in desperation, I have sometimes resorted to the old chestnut: If you were to be shot in an hour's time, and were given the opportunity of preaching one last sermon, what would your theme be? The answers I have received have

16. Recounted by A. J. Grieve, "Christian Learning and Christian Living," *The Congregational Year Book 1937*, 80. This is Grieve's address from the Chair of the Congregational Union of England and Wales, delivered in the City Temple, London, on 12 May 1936.

17. See Lockley, *Early Congregationalism in Queensland*, 124–25.

18. D. R. Peel, *Ministry for Mission*, 121.

not been uniformly encouraging. David Peel's experience has evidently been even more hair-raising: "It seems that God waits until a professional person is about to get a lucrative early-retirement package before calling them to ministry! I have noticed also how often non-stipendiary ministers apply for stipendiary service at the point they are made redundant."[19] Of second-career candidates for ordination, Leslie Houlden has surmised that for some, "Ordination is . . . a route to individual fulfilment, freeing them from restrictions which their previous employment imposed."[20] I fear that if such persons have no other motivation they may find, not individual fulfilment, but rather that they have jumped out of the frying pan into the fire. It is small comfort, but in 1900 D. W. Simon, then of Yorkshire United Independent College, Bradford, wrote a letter in which he said of his students, "I fear the vast majority are going out into the ministry without any definite conviction as to the reason why they are ministers: certainly not that it is their supreme business to *convert*. At the utmost it is 'to do good'—which often means entertaining and interesting, with a little mild piety thrown in."[21] "How great an evil it is," the Presbyterian divine, John Flavel, rightly declared "to intrude into the office of the ministry without a due call."[22]

It is sometimes even more difficult to obtain an answer to the question, Why do you wish to be a minister of The United Reformed Church? I have heard answers along the lines of "Because I was brought up in it" or, "Because I have found my local church friendly." The fact that we are a people who have a pneumatological *cum* ecclesiological *raison d'être*, a way of working out our convictions in terms of church order, insights to bring to the ecumenical table, and a witness to make in relation to the state, all too often seems to have passed some enquirers by. The "pious young men" who sought entry to Blackburn Independent[23] Academy (1816) were left in no doubt as to what was required of them. It was resolved that

> each should be required to bring before the Committee, from the church to which he belonged, a testimonial to the suitableness of his character and qualifications, and that he present in writing a

19. D. R. Peel, *Ministry for Mission*, 120.

20. Houlden, "Education in Theology," 173.

21. Powicke, *David Worthington Simon*, 229.

22. Flavel, *Works*, I, 94.

23. The terms "Independent" and "Congregational" were current from the 1640s onwards. The former refers to the stand taken in relation to the Church of England "by law established," the latter to the favoured polity.

brief account of his views of Divine truth, of his religious experience, and of the motives which induce him to enter into the Christian Ministry; that he then deliver a short address; after which, and subsequent conversation, if he be approved, he shall be received for six months; and if he continue to give satisfaction, at the expiration of that period he shall be fully admitted.[24]

By the time I applied for entry to Blackburn Academy's successor, Lancashire Independent College (1843–1958) candidates were expected to have had two years of preaching experience in the churches, and were required to sit entrance examinations in "English Bible" and "The History and Principles of Congregationalism." This, I thought, and still feel, was all to the good—though I should now substitute "The United Reformed Church" for "Congregationalism."[25] If people are to be formed for ministry and not simply primed with the theological disciplines, there is much to be said for their being "traditioned" from the outset of their courses. Once our candidates are accepted for the ministry their call is further tested through a programme of education. I shall have more to say about this in my final chapter.

I underline the fact that the ministry of the gospel is a high calling, a vocation. Indeed, I feel I must labour the point because I find that in some quarters the fact is misunderstood and even denied. To put it bluntly, there are those who see the ministry as a job. In the course of my globe-trotting I have from time to time come across ministers of the gospel who think in terms of ministerial "career patterns," which generally seems to mean moving up the scale to a higher salary and a taller steeple. This sometimes goes hand in hand with a corporate view of the church in which all is presided over by a Senior Executive Minister, who is "over" a staff of assistant ministers, some of whom have specialist roles. Thus I have met a "Minister for preaching and administration," which conjures up the vision of a poor soul sitting in an office all the week arranging things, and emerging on Sundays to preach to people he or she has never met, and of whose pastoral and other needs he or she is quite unaware. Then there was the church of "affluent 'fast-track' commuters" who were advertising for a Senior Executive Pastor, to "design and build infrastructure, envision and create ministry

24. Slate, *A Brief History of the Rise and Progress of the Lancashire Congregational Union*, 120.

25. "What was the Great Ejectment all about?" Too many ministers asked me that question during 2012, the 350th anniversary year of that significant event in our history. It was disquieting.

delivery teams" and so forth: "Seminary degree unnecessary and a business background preferred."[26] And I recall very clearly the elder who told me of his church's wonderful new system of ministry. I pricked up my ears, hoping to learn of a theological breakthrough. I was more than somewhat deflated when he said with considerable glee, "In this church we have one called minister and five contract ministers; and the beauty of the contract ones is that we can fire them so easily."

In The United Reformed Church we do not have the temptations of numerical size and funds (nor, indeed, do most pastorates in the North America), and so I grant at once that it is not so easy for ministers and members of The United Reformed Church to think in the terms I have just described. But I have encountered a few who make the effort, otherwise I would not have recounted my exotic experiences as a caution. In our case there has been a dramatic levelling of stipends as compared with former years, and this should make it easier for the Holy Spirit to call ministers to the less "fashionable" places.[27] Certainly it is some years since I heard anyone say "Now that $x$ has gone to $y$ church, there's nowhere else for him to go," albeit there were always inner city and village churches to which the silver-haired princes of the pulpit could have gone. What I sometimes hear today is talk from ministers about hours worked per week. I am told that they are not on call at all times. Some even hanker after formal contracts. It is almost as if they are on the way to thinking of themselves as employees of the Church which, theologically at least, they are not. This is why I spoke of a stipend, not a salary. A stipendiary minister is one who is expected by others to perform certain duties, but who, apart from some fixed points such as times of services, is given latitude to arrange the work according to his or her own priorities. In the old phrase, the minister's stipend was designed to free him (they were all male in those days) from worldly care (something which by no means always happened) in order that he might devote full-time service to Christ. R. W. Hamilton was clear on the matter in 1845: "The Congregational ministry, though most properly alienated from trade, through an appointment held apart from the business of life, is in no sense a profession. . . . [T]he ministers of our creed and discipline do

---

26. If you can bear it, see *Christianity Today*, 22 May 2000, 107.

27. Though there is some reason to think that the Holy Spirit's advantage in this respect is in some cases cancelled out by the fact that increasingly two spouses work, and one may not wish, or be easily able, to move.

not of themselves constitute an order."[28] Sixty years on, Forsyth was more specific. The minister

> is not the servant, not the employee, of the Church. He is an apostle to it, the mouthpiece of Christ's gospel to it, the servant of the Word and not of the Church; he serves the Church only for that sake. The ministry is a prophetic sacramental office; it is not secretarial, it is not merely presidential. It is sacramental and not merely functional. It is the outward and visible agent of the inward gospel of grace.[29]

Roughly a century on, a wise pastor lamented, "More and more it seems that the very life and nature of the church has succumbed to the understanding that the church is a service agency providing religious goods and services to consumers hungry for spirituality and clergy are hired to provide those goods and services."[30]

This quotation makes it clear that it is not only ministers and those enquiring about the ministry who may be at sea regarding the nature of the calling, but church members also may be mightily confused. It has for long been our practice that both ministers and pastorates should consider one vacancy at a time only. This is not simply in order to avoid unseemly competition between ministers; more importantly it is to honour our principle that at Church Meeting, and in the concurring council,[31] we seek the mind of Christ and unanimity in him (something about which I shall have more to say later), and that this objective is needlessly complicated if church members are torn between a list of ministers, and ministers between a list of vacancies. Let us therefore pay heed to another true tale that has become part of our folk memory. It concerns Principal A. J. Grieve, sometime of Lancashire Independent College, Manchester. One day he received a letter from the secretary of a fashionable vacant church, who had been instructed

---

28. Hamilton, "On the Importance of drawing into the Ministry pious and devoted Young Men," in *Minutes of the Proceedings of a Conference of Delegates from the Committees of Various Theological Colleges*, 26. The conference was held at the Congregational Library, Blomfield Street, London.

29. Forsyth, *The Church and the Sacraments*, 132–33.

30. Roth, "Who Will Serve?" 3.

31. I am here primarily concerned with the role of the local church in addressing a call to a minister. I shall discuss the wider councils of The United Reformed Church in Appendix 2, while Church Meeting will be considered in the following chapter because the conduct of it constitutes an important part of the regular work of ministers in pastoral charge.

to write to four of the college principals in the following terms: "Our pastorate is vacant, and I am writing to four principals to invite them to send their three best men to preach in turn with a view. When we have heard all twelve, we shall make our selection." Grieve, who was famous for his sharp wit and his one-liners on postcards, replied entirely appropriately, "The Christian ministry is a vocation, not a race meeting, and no students will be coming from this college."[32] Many a church when contemplating addressing a call to a minister would do well to answer Forsyth's question, "Is he for you a minister of the Gospel, or of your ideals, tastes, affections, and idiosyncrasies?"[33]

At the present time, as is well known, The United Reformed Church faces considerable challenges regarding financial resources and competent personnel. With a view to apportioning scarce resources as equitably as possible we have for some years now thought in terms of the deployment of ministers. I simply enter a plea that we take care not to allow deployment to trump vocation. There is everything to be said for a group of churches in one pastorate meeting as one Church Meeting to address a call to a minister. I am sure I am not the only person who, when each of the several churches within a group has independently pronounced upon a prospective minister, has later heard rumblings to the effect that "We didn't want him/her, but the others in the group outvoted us." But what happens when a pastorate with a settled minister is invited to take another church under its wing? I should like to think that such a minister would receive a call from the bereft church, which he or she would be entitled to accept or decline. The reason is that no church should be regularly served by one whom they

32. From time to time letters appear in *Reform* which exhort us to be more business-like in the matter of "appointing" our ministers to vacant pastorates, so that vacancies will be shorter. However much good business practice may assist us in other aspects of churchly life, it would seem that where calls to ministerial service are concerned "more business-like" sometimes means "less theological."

33. Forsyth, *The Church, the Gospel and Society*, 85. A further issue which sometimes arises not only when ministers are to be called (or not), but on other significant occasions, is the position of absentee church members. In such circumstances I have heard requests for proxy voting. But (a) we are not in the business of voting, but of seeking the mind of Christ, under the guidance of the Holy Spirit, *together*. (b) Absentees are not in a position to have their opinions refined or radically altered, because they are not within earshot of the proceedings. (c) However, it is perfectly in order for those unable to be present to communicate their views in writing to the Meeting, and such views should be made known to the gathered saints, provided that written judgments be understood as for information only, and that the discernment of the mind of Christ remains the responsibility of those gathered.

have not called; and every minister is entitled to know that he or she has been called by the people whom they regularly serve. When such a call is given and accepted, induction into ministry in the "added" church should follow. As John Robinson, the pastor to the Pilgrims, rightly declared, "The bond between the minister, and people is the most strait, and near religious bond that may be, and therefore not to be entered but with mutual consent, any more than the civil bond of marriage between the husband, and wife."[34]

Then there is the question how far we do well to advertise pastoral and denominational vacancies. This can be another way of introducing the element of inter-ministerial competition, thereby seeming to diminish the idea of a call. Again, it leaves the initiative with the minister rather than with the church, and may encourage talk of ministerial "job-hunting"—a demeaning term indeed. One might also ruefully observe that we do not have so many ministers that between them the Synod Moderators are utterly at a loss as to whom to approach regarding pastoral and other denominational vacancies. On the other hand, advertisements are an efficient way of letting those who may be interested, and might be overlooked, know of vacancies. Even then, however, I think it well—whether a pastoral, college or denominational post is in view—that the responsible body remember that it is concerned with a call, not merely with an appointment to a post, and hence that only one candidate at a time is considered.

Finally under this heading, it must be confessed that within our tradition we have not always known what to do with ministers who pursue a call other than one to a pastorate (even though in the seventeenth century John Owen was able to approve of itinerant evangelists who worked for the conversion of souls). We have had ministers serving in chaplaincies to the forces, hospitals and industry; the British and Foreign Bible Society; the BBC and ITV; higher education and school teaching; and social work, synod and ecumenical posts, to name but a few. We have also in the past sent numerous missionaries overseas, and these were normally commissioned for service in their home churches or in the pastorate they were leaving. But those in the former list have not been commissioned. I believe that, as a matter of good church order and ministerial discipline, those who feel a call to a sphere other than a pastorate, ought first to take it to the church—which in my case has always meant the regional moderator. I was not required to do this, but I felt that I am a minister not for my sake but for the sake of Christ and his church, and it mattered to the church how I

---

34. Robinson, *Works*, II, 396.

was exercising my calling. I may say that in every case I was encouraged to proceed. I have crusaded on this point over the years, and I understand that those sensing such calls are nowadays expected to follow such a path. I am not sure, however, whether they are always formally commissioned for service in spheres where induction as we understand it in pastorates is either not possible or is inappropriate, though I hope that they are.

## THE CHARACTER OF THE MINISTER

Much could be said under this heading, but I shall be selective. I fully grant that the following points are so obvious that they hardly need to be written down. But if the minister really is to be one in whom others can see something of Christ, it is not irrelevant to indicate what this may mean in terms of the minister's character. I have not ranked the following characteristics on a scale on relative importance: they are all important, and I set them down in no particular order.

First, ministers are called to be persons of integrity, by which I mean honest, trustworthy, and not hypocritical. We should not claim an experience that we do not possess. The evangelist Brownlow North cautioned ministerial students "to beware of becoming *cumberers of the ground*, for such we would certainly be, if we ventured forth to the holy ministry unconverted."[35] John Brown of Haddington, the Associate Synod's professor, underlined the point: "To commend a Saviour one has no love for; to preach a Gospel one does not believe; to point out the way to heaven, and never to have taken one step that way; to enforce a saving acquaintance with religion and to be an entire stranger to it oneself, how sad, how preposterous!"[36] Chaucer's poor parson, who is introduced to us in the Prologue to *The Canterbury Tales*, provides a counter example, for

> Christes lore and his apostles twelve

> He taught, and first he followed it himself.

I do not overlook the fact that in the ambiguities of life as we have to live it our integrity can be assailed in a variety of ways. I recall, for example, a kindly minister whose great aim was to spread peace abroad and keep the saints from one another's throats. In the course of his pastoral visits prior to

35. Moody-Stuart, *Brownlow North*, 165.
36. Mackenzie, *John Brown of Haddington*, 138.

Church Meeting he would meet those on either side of a proposed policy, and he would agree with both parties in their homes. Come the Church Meeting, both factions would claim his support, with the result that the members found it increasingly hard to believe what he said.

Nor should we overlook the shadow side of integrity, which is that dogmatic, inflexible rigidity which will brook no opposition or consider an alternative view. I was stunned to be told by a hard-line Calvinist biblical inerrantist minister that it had taken him two years to strip the membership roll of unbelievers, but now, at last, he could begin to build a true church. He seemed to have overlooked the fact that in setting out to guard the faith he was usurping the role of God the Holy Spirit, and that both winnowing and upbuilding are the work of the church's Lord, who is not helped by arrogant, bullying, loveless, ministers. As William Cowper put it, "If a man has great and good news to tell me, he will not do it angrily, and in much heat and discomposure of spirit. It is not therefore easy to conceive, on what ground a scolding Minister can justify a conduct, which only proves, that he does not understand his errand."[37]

This leads directly to the second consideration, namely, that ministers should guard against false pride and arrogance, and should pray for genuine humility. There should be no lording it over the flock, for Christ the Lord took a towel and washed his disciples' feet—the task of a servant. All the saints, but especially ministers in their exemplary role, should seek grace to live a holy life, which is the life of deepest joy, not of doleful morbidity. Of Highland ministers it was said that "It was neither by talents, nor by learning, nor by oratory, nor was it by all these together, that a leading place was attained by the ministers in the Highlands; but by a profound experience of the power of godliness, a clear view of the doctrines of grace, peculiar nearness to God, a holy life, and a blessed ministry."[38] It can still happen that "People are proud of their minister, not for what he is in heart, but because he is more learned, more eloquent, more naturally capable, than other preachers in the same town. It is a pity when ministers themselves . . . are content to have it so."[39] With special reference to the minister's pastoral work that exemplary moderator, W. J. Coggan, wrote, "A true pastor must undertake fearless examination, a constant humble self-analysis; he must be ready to acknowledge his own shortcomings and needs, and to submit

---

37. Quoted by Bridges, *The Christian Ministry*, 333.
38. Kennedy, *The Days of the Fathers in Ross-shire*, 19.
39. Denney, *The Second Epistle to the Corinthians*, 189.

his achievements and ambitions to the disinfecting and therapeutic process of true humour and the searching standards of the Gospels if he is to be indeed a healer of the souls of others."[40]

Finally, ministers need to be disciplined stewards of their time. Sad to say, some are lazy. When I was told that a minister was pleased to have the care of four or five churches because it enabled him always to be somewhere else, I was not impressed. Indeed, the parson we hear of in George Crabbe's *The Village* sprang at once to mind. He was

> A jovial youth, who thinks his Sunday task
> As much as God or man can fairly ask;
> The rest he gives to loves and labours light,
> To fields the morning, and to feasts the night . . .
> A sportsman keen, he shoots through half the day,
> And, skill'd at whist, devotes the night to play:
> Then, while such honours bloom around his head,
> Shall he sit sadly by the sick man's bed,
> To raise the hope he feels not, or with zeal
> To combat fears that e'en the pious feel?

At the opposite extreme are compulsively conscientious ministers who work themselves to a frazzle, as if the *parousia* would be delayed if they so much as took an evening off. Even Richard Baxter, than whom few ministers were more conscientious in all the duties pertaining to their role, somewhat grudgingly conceded that a student's recreations "must be as whetting is with the mower, that is only to be used so far as is necessary to his work."[41] Are some ministers flogging themselves because they are attempting to hold the pastorate (whether single or multi-church) together single-handedly? If so, why is this? Is it because they need to be in control, or is it because the church members are not willing, or are not being encouraged, to offer their several ministries? Is it that some ministers have heard so many mutterings to the effect that "The church used to be full when I was young" that they feel it is their task to fill it up again—in which case they need to heed C. H. Spurgeon's advice: "[The Lord] will not blame you for not doing that which is beyond your mental power or physical strength, You are required to be faithful, but you are not bound

---

40. Coggan, "The Minister as Pastor," 110.

41. Baxter, *Gildas Salvianus; The Reformed Pastor*, 394.

to be successful."[42] Both in pastoral charge and during my itinerant ministry I have been informed that "When I was young this church was full." This was sometimes coded language for, "Why are you not (or why is our minister not) filling it up now?" On a few sample occasions I compared the membership of the churches fifty years before with the number of seats available, and discovered that in no case did the membership ever exceed one quarter of the seats. Thus the members' memories either were of special occasions—church and Sunday school anniversaries and the like; or those who used to fill the pews did so perhaps because church was warmer than home; or because employers said or implied, "If you work in my factory you attend my church."

The upshot is that ministers stand among the saints as those who serve, but they are not servile dogsbodies. It is tragic that in some cases ministers are attempting both to keep the churchly show on the road, and at the same time stand in for the members as the main witness to, and servant of, the wider society. The costs can be great: ministerial burnout; the extinguishing of "the spirit of prayer [which] cannot breathe freely in the atmosphere of constant and exciting employment";[43] and the skimping of pulpit preparation, with the result that "You have bustle all the week and baldness all the Sunday."[44]

## THE CHALLENGES OF THE MINISTRY

Many of the challenges faced by ministers have already been alluded to, but something remains to be said. It is not beyond the saints to be obstreperous. Legend has it that when a deacon suggested that the church might apply on the financially-pressed minister's behalf to the Lady Hewley Charity's fund for "poor and godly ministers," a fellow deacon retorted, "God will make him godly, and we'll keep him poor." When James Rattray was called to the Mixenden pastorate in 1791 the church found that his ardent Calvinism was not to their taste. He is said to have been "starved out."[45] Again, in 1864 Thomas Jenkins of St. Davids, Wales, accepted the pastorate of Ipswich, New South Wales. All did not go well, and in 1867 he resigned, pointing out in a letter that the church "has no right to get quit of him by insufficient salary. . . . I am

42. Spurgeon, *An All-Round Ministry*, 214.

43. Bridges, *The Christian Ministry*, 145.

44. Forsyth, *Positive Preaching and the Modern Mind*, 117.

45. Miall, *Congregationalism in Yorkshire*, 319.

sorry that actions are deemed respectable in religious affairs whose meanness would be considered disgusting in commercial transactions."[46]

Again, some saints, on being greeted at church or in the street by the minister, have a very accusing way of responding to a polite, "How are you?" by saying, "I'm better *now*"—as if to say, "Where were you when I was ill?" At the end of a poem about Mrs. Huff, who was "up in the miff tree" because the rector had not visited her whereas the doctor had, the rector enquires:

> Then I asked her how the doctor
> Knew that sickness laid her low;
> And she said that she had called him
> On the phone and told him so . . .
> Now the doctor gets his bill paid
> With a nicely written cheque,
> But the Rector, for not knowing,
> Simply gets it in the neck.[47]

The sternest passage I have ever read in a charge to the church at an ordination service was written by Bernard Lord Manning, a son of the manse, an historian, and probably Congregationalism's most perceptive lay theologian of the twentieth century:

> No minister worth the name wants an easy job. . . . Some hard things a minister accepts: a bare living wage or less, the cold shoulder of the fashionable world, the indifference and inattention of the world at large, the scorn of the successful, the insolence of the social climber. . . . He expects . . . to be patronized by the vulgarian, to be set right by fools, to be gossiped about by the feather-brained, to have his work spoilt by the spiteful. . . . This for Christ's sake he can bear. . . . But what no young man who has put his whole life on the altar can expect . . . is the coldness, the callousness, the deadness of those to whom he looks for help . . . it is when he sees the abomination of desolation standing where it ought not—indifference, worldliness, heartlessness in you the Body of Christ, it is then that the cold fear paralyses his soul. . . . If this be Christ's Body, it is a dead body, and Christ is dead. . . . In such an hour the

---

46. Lockley, *Early Congregationalism in Queensland*, 41.

47. Anon., *World Christian Digest*, June 1953, 60.

Saviour can still save His servant, but do you envy the Church that plunges a man into that pit?[48]

The prevention of such calamitous situations, and the resolution of them when they occur, is usually a complex matter. In general terms it may be that some unfortunate situations could be avoided if more searching discussion were held prior to the addressing and acceptance of a call; and that others might be resolved if either the minister or people, or both, had more realistic expectations of one another. Even the wise pastor, Richard Baxter, was probably being over-optimistic when he declared that "If God would but reform the ministry, and set them on their duties zealously and faithfully, the people would certainly be reformed."[49] "Certainly"? No necessary cause-and-effect operates in this realm, and I fear it is not impossible for saintly toes to be dug in against any such happy outcome. Be that as it may, enough has been said to show both that the challenge of loving the saints for Christ's sake whilst not liking some of them very much can be stringent indeed, and that the saints, in fidelity to their ministry, have no right to shelve their responsibility of upholding and, where necessary, ministering to the one they have called into their midst.

By way of a footnote on the issue of stress in ministers, I was concerned to learn that an American sociological survey had revealed that "Pastors found it difficult to confide their problems in denominational leaders because they did not want to jeopardize future calls and promotion." There are two problems here: the stress, and the word "promotion" which, in my view, has no place in talk of ministry, for one cannot be promoted when one has already been honoured with the highest vocation imaginable, no matter in what sphere it is being exercised. Again, the pastors could not confide in their ministerial peers "because of the enormous competition that exists among them."[50] How very sad. I also note that over against consumerist models of success, Christopher Beeley of Yale Divinity School is quoted as saying that "the spiritual condition of the flock is the only real measure of a leader's success."[51] But (a) Since there is no known measure for measuring this condition, how would a minister know whether or not he or she had

48. Manning, *A Layman in the Ministry*, 156–57.

49. Baxter, *Autobiography* (abridged), 97.

50. Dart, "Stressed Out," 8. The research was undertaken by Dean R. Hoge and Jacqueline E. Wenger.

51. Review of Beeley, *Leading God's People: Wisdom from the Early Church for Today*, by Anthony B. Johnson, 40.

been "successful"? (b) Is not a minister who supposes that his or her task is to enhance the spiritual condition of the flock needlessly manufacturing stress—not to mention usurping the role of God the Holy Spirit who alone takes the scales from people's eyes? (c) Are we not on a slippery slope at the bottom of which stands the hapless faith missionary who is expected to show that in the month just passed more converts materialized than in the same month in the previous year—a strangely "commercial" requirement which calls to mind Tesco rather than the kingdom of God. Ministers carry enough responsibility in being faithful and obedient to Christ; they do not need to carry the additional burden of self- or other-imposed false expectations.

Whether their despondency is caused from within or without, how might ministers respond to it? The Presbyterian divine and Dissenting academy tutor, Henry Grove, delivered a sermon on 7 October 1730 on the occasion of the ordination of his nephew Thomas Amory and his friend William Cornish. The text is Philippians 1: 21, and the title of the sermon is "On Living for Christ." Grove's theme is that

> every faithful Minister makes it the principal scope and business of his life to promote the honour and interest of his Redeemer; more particularly in the salvation of those souls that are commited [sic] to his charge—that in preaching the Gospel, and all other parts of his ministerial conduct and labours, he follows that method which he apprehends to be best adapted to the attainment of this glorious end—and, finally, that he esteems the approbation of his Lord, by whom he was bought, and is imployed, an ample recompence for all the discouragements and self-denial he can undergo in his service.[52]

Many from many Christian traditions have endorsed these words, among them Thomas Scott (1747–1821), the Bible commentator and a founder of the Church Missionary Society: "With all my discouragements and sinful despondency; in my better moments, I can think of no work worth doing compared with this. Had I a thousand lives, I would willingly spend them all in it; and had I as many sons, I should gladly devote them to it."[53] John Brown was similarly minded. In an address of 1782 he exhorted his theological students thus:

---

52. Grove, *Ethical and Theological Writings*, I, 512–13.

53. Scott, *Life of the Rev Thomas Scott, D.D.*, 242.

Believe this on the testimony of God Himself; believe it on the testimony of all His faithful servants; and, if mine were of any avail, I should add it, that there is no *Master* so kind as Christ, no *service* so pleasant and profitable as that of Christ, and no *reward* so full, satisfying, and permanent as that of Christ. Let us, therefore, begin all things from Christ; carry on all things with and through Christ; and let all things aim at, and end, in Christ. "Christ is all in all."[54]

Here is the eschatological hope, the strongest consolation that any minister of the gospel, and any ministering saint, could possibly have.

54. Mackenzie, *John Brown of Haddington*, 140–41.

# 3

# The Work of the Ministry
## (1) The Worship of the Church

IN A SERMON ENTITLED, "Faithfulness unto Death," Henry Roberts Reynolds, declared that it "is impossible to exaggerate the responsibilities of one who essays to become a messenger and apostle of Christ."[1] In this chapter I shall focus upon the minister's responsibilities as these relate to leading public worship, and in the next I shall turn to the preaching of the gospel, and the offering of pastoral care.

The first duty of the church is the worship of God, and if ever we are tempted to think of public worship as being something routine and lacklustre, let us remind ourselves that it is well nigh miraculous that sinners are called by the God of holy and pursuing love to commune with him in concert. The first task—or, rather, the high, unmerited, privilege—of the minister of the gospel is to lead the saints to the throne of grace. For much of our history this would have been taken for granted, but I emphasise it now because, from their characteristic attitudes and actions, one could be forgiven for suspecting that some churches and some ministers think that the church exists primarily to be a social service, or an agent for social and political change, or an hospitable place where the needy may find friendship and a cup of tea. There is nothing wrong with any of this, but it should be prompted and inspired by the church's worship and it should not take precedence over it, otherwise we have put the cart before the horse.

---

1. Reynolds, *Notes on the Christian Life*, 353.

The story of worship in the traditions which comprise The United Reformed Church is varied indeed, and I cannot give an account of it here.[2] What the record shows is that public worship has undergone numerous changes over time; that here our worship has been more "formal," there more "charismatic"; and that it took too long for women to be welcomed as leaders of it.

Where public worship is concerned a very important principle is at stake, and it is one to which all ministers should pay due heed. Public worship is the worship of the people. It is not the showcase for the minister's pet theories, aesthetic ideals, favourite hymns, dramatic prowess, or private prayers. In preaching and in the blessing ministers stand as apostles of Christ before the people; in praise and prayer they stand with the people, making a common offering to the Lord of all; but in both cases they stand as public persons, for the gospel is not their private possession, it belongs to the church; and the worship is the response of the church to the gospel. Moreover, when Christians gather for worship they "do not grope after an unknown God. We worship that which we do know—for ours is a God who has revealed Himself in His mighty acts. Our worship is a glorifying of His Name by the celebration or rehearsal of those mighty acts, culminating in the Incarnation, Death, and Resurrection of Christ."[3] In other words, we worship one who has graciously made himself known to us as one whose active, saving love is as holy as it is merciful, who delights in the praise of the saints, and who is ever ready to forgive the sins of the penitent. All of this is proclaimed in the church's worship, both in words and in sacramental actions.

Some forms of worship may appeal more to us than others but, granted the sincerity of it, we dare not say that God is displeased with it (however much it may irritate some liturgiologists). Worship may properly be offered in homes, hospitals, around camp fires, and in many other places, but I maintain that there is a continuing place for the "full diet" of Word and sacrament. This service is comprehensive as to its parts, and it is dialogical in nature: God calls us to worship, we approach God, God addresses us in his Word, we respond to God in thanksgiving. The Bible is literally central, and when the Lord's Supper is kept we have the enacted witness to the gospel which was verbally proclaimed. The following is the bare bones of such

2. I have written on "The Worship of English Congregationalism" in *Testimony and Tradition*, ch.2.

3. Cocks, "Lectures on Preaching, II," Cocks papers, Dr. Williams's Library, London.

a service, and with it, I am sure, many members of The United Reformed Church are familiar. One might call it a classical order in that it reaches back to the worship of the early church with its liturgy of the catechumens (up to the sacrament) followed by the sacramental liturgy of the faithful; and hence the shape of the service is of some ecumenical significance.

## The Approach

The call to worship in sentences of Scripture

Hymn

Prayers of adoration, confession, and supplication

## The Ministry of the Word

Reading from the Old Testament

Hymn/Metrical Psalm

Reading from the Epistles

Reading from the Gospels

Hymn

The sermon

## The Response to the Gospel

Hymn

The offering

The Lord's Supper including the Lord's Prayer; or Prayers of thanksgiving and intercession, and the Lord's Prayer

Hymn

The Blessing

Before proceeding further I pause to observe that through the ages public worship, which should be a sublime experience, has been a source of irritation as well, and this for a variety of reasons. We shall see how people have taken up sides on prayers, hymns and music, readings and, no doubt, William Cowper stands for others in the list of irritants which he supplied:

> I could wish that the clergy would inform their congregations, that there is no occasion to scream themselves hoarse in making the responses; that the town-crier is not the only person qualified to pray with due devotion; and that he who bawls loudest may nevertheless be the wickedest fellow in the parish. The old women too in the aisle might be told, that their time would be better employed in

attending to the sermon, than in fumbling over their tattered tes-
taments till they have found the text; by which time the discourse
is near drawing to a conclusion: while a word or two of instruction
might not be thrown away upon the younger part of the congregation, to teach them that making posies in summer time, and
cracking nuts in autumn, is no part of the religious ceremony.[4]

So to a few remarks on the components of the outlined service, whilst
reserving the subject of preaching to the following chapter. For almost
twenty years my wife and I worked away from England. On our return
we discovered that during our absence The United Reformed Church had
made two liturgical discoveries. The first was how to open worship with a
cheery "Good morning everybody!" The second was how to erect screens
on which to project words to be sung. I shall say more about the latter
shortly, but now I wish to enter a plea for allowing the Bible to have the first
word by way of a call to worship. I suspect that the cheery greeting, sometimes accompanied by a broad grin in "Wake up, happy campers!" style, is
designed to make people feel welcome and comfortable and, indeed, they
should be warmly greeted as they enter the church. But then they should
compose themselves for the business in hand, and the next words they hear
should be scriptural. If the minister intrudes in a feel-good manner we are
already on the way to losing the sense of reverence and holy awe: we have
come to do business with God. Indeed, it is possible to infer something of
the minister's doctrine of God from the way in which he or she arrives, or
bounds, into the church. While nobody wishes the saints to feel uncomfort-
able, one might gently suggest that too much comfort may be out of place
until after the prayer of confession! In one of the best known passages of
the Old Testament Isaiah of Jerusalem has a vision of God who is at once
transcendent—"high and lifted up" and also, uncomfortably, close, so that
penitence was required (Isa 6:1–8). I am sometimes tempted to wonder
whether, when the saints gather for worship in our churches, they are encouraged to feel that they are in the presence of such a God. There is a
reverential medium between a happy hour and an hour sitting in a freezer.

Then we come to the hymns. In our tradition these are particularly
important as enabling the participation of the people in worship, and over
the centuries our hymn writers, from Watts and Doddridge, through Joseph Hart and Josiah Conder, to Elvet Lewis and Alan Gaunt have made

---

4. Cowper, "Mr. Village to Mr. Town," from *The Connoisseur* 134 (19 August 1756); in
Chalmers, *The British Essayists*, XXVI, 360.

an enduring contribution to the worship of the church at large. We may perhaps take it for granted that ministers would find it difficult to ignore the major seasons of the Christian Year in their selection of hymns, but, more generally, I have always felt it appropriate to vary the hymns within a service by content, metre, and style. Thus, for example, a hymn of praise, or one calling the saints to worship, might well be the first to be sung. While it is appropriate that the hymn following the sermon should reinforce the message delivered (and Philip Doddridge wrote many of his hymns for precisely that purpose), it is not necessary, or even desirable, that every hymn should be on the theme for the day, for we are concerned with the worship of the people, and the concerns of many of them may be accommodated, for example, by a hymn on prayer, or one which encourages discipleship. As to metre, it is surprising how five hymns in the same metre can make for a certain dullness in the service. Where style is concerned the thoughtful minister will not choose five unison hymns, lest those whose vocal range restricts them to the alto or bass line in four part harmony are excluded from singing altogether.

I was taught that the architecture of the church should be informed by the doctrine of the church, and that on entering the building one's eye should be drawn to the most significant objects: the open Bible, the pulpit, table, and font (or portable "fonticule"!). I find that today my eye is sometimes drawn to a pulpit-obscuring projection screen and a drum kit; and on one occasion, had a kindly saxophonist not loaned me his music stand I should have had nowhere to place my sermon notes. Now what is going on? I think that we miss a great deal if in the "full diet" of worship we obscure those objects that speak most directly of God's address to us in Word and sacraments: especially so if this is done in the interests of an occasion which more closely resembles a raucous, upbeat, gig than a joyous celebration of the holy God of all grace and mercy.

As to music in the service: we may easily err in either of two directions where hymns are concerned. On the one hand, there are those who have what may be described as refined musical tastes, and they can be prone to certain prejudices as a result. I recall that Erik Routley, our well-known hymnologist, did not like tunes which began with the same three notes—of which there are numerous examples, from "Arizona" to "Whitburn"; and he was on the shadow side of complimentary where the tunes of Stainer were concerned. But if a hymn is a unit comprising tune and matching words, I think that we should take care not to be artistically precious. I would not object if on occasion people wondered whether their anchor would hold, or whether they should be rescuing the perishing; and, provided that they are not over-used, a hymn more suited to personal devotion—such as "Jesus, Saviour, pilot me" (which I once heard memorably rendered by the Filey Fishermen's Choir, founded in 1823)—may bring hope to some. I sometimes feel inclined to select the thoroughly biblical hymn "I'm but a stranger here, Heaven is my home" by way of reminding all concerned of an important doctrine about which we hear too little, except at those funeral services in which the achievements of the deceased have not altogether displaced the gospel.

On the other hand, there are the many relatively recently written popular songs that find their way onto projection screens in these technologically-enlightened times, and these have been the occasion of the worship wars that some churches have endured, and by which not a few have been split. I feel that here, too, we need to discriminate before being tempted to denounce all such offerings, for they come in many different styles. There are, for example, original songs which follow closely the biblical text, which has not been forced within particular metres as sometimes happened in the traditional metrical psalms: "I joy'd when to the house of God, Go up, they said, to me" (Ps 122: 1). Then there are contributions in the style of country and western music: "My wife has left me, my son's gone off the rails, somebody's run over the cat, and I'm a dreadful sinner." It would be quite wrong to suggest that this sort of composition might be defined as "Job meets Mills and Boon, with banjo accompaniment," but at least it is not feel-good sentiment. Nor should we make the mistake of supposing that there is no doctrine in recent offerings. I learn, for example, that the Calvinist hip-hop artist, Flame, who hails from Louisville, can be surprisingly technical, as when he denounces modalistic monarchianism: "That's not the Scriptures, that's confusion, And it takes stabs at the hypostatic union."[5] Shades of the line in the seventh-century hymn, "Christ is made the sure foundation," translated from the Latin by John Mason Neale, "Consubstantial, co-eternal while unending ages run."

But when one has entered all appropriate caveats, and been as gracious as possible, there remains a significant problem. It is that so many of the songs are banal, self-serving, and boringly repetitive. They should be

---

5. In the interests of the unity (monarchy) of God, the modalistic monarchians held that there were successive modes of being within the Godhead, thereby disallowing the independent subsistence of the Son. Sabellius was a prominent exponent of this doctrine, and "Sabellianism" is an alternative name for it.

very sparingly used, if used at all; otherwise any hope that Nonconformists will continue to learn their doctrine from their hymns (as could once be said with some justification) is vain indeed. I must at once concede that in every generation Christians live amidst the ephemeral where hymns are concerned. Charles Wesley wrote more than six thousand hymns, of which thirty-two only are found in *Rejoice and Sing*. Isaac Watts was not above perpetrating godly doggerel (which can make a point but does not always stand the test of time); and the pioneer Baptist hymn writer, Benjamin Keach, wrote some four hundred hymns of which, to the best of my knowledge, none are found in current mainline hymnals. What concerns me is that a diet of the type of songs I am now considering is all that many Christians know. I have come across church-attending Christians in their forties who simply do not know the great hymns of the church. One who has written on "The Juvenilization of the Church" has concluded that it "tends to create a self-centered, emotionally driven, and intellectually empty faith"[6] such that adults are apparently happy to be adolescents once more. This is truly disturbing. What of the young people themselves? On more than one occasion, I have been told that bright and breezy music played with gusto and volume will act as bait to bring young people to church. This is a huge assumption concerning the tastes of young people, who know when they are being patronized, and can be better served.[7] It would seem to be the case, however, that in a service of any kind, if the music and words convey the impression that being a Christian is about little more than being constantly jolly, then a wide range of human emotions and needs (such as we find in the Psalms) are left out of account. There is a holy joy; there is a comprehensive repertoire; there is a godly reverence. As long ago as 1923, the distinguished Congregational minister, J. H. Jowett, wrote,

> We leave our places of worship, and no deep inexpressible wonder sits upon our faces. We can sing these lilting melodies, and when we go out into the streets our faces are one with the faces of those who have left theatres and the music halls. There is nothing about us to suggest that we have been looking at anything stupendous and overwhelming. . . . That is the element we are losing, and its

6. Bergler, "When are we Going to Grow Up? 23. As for the increasingly ubiquitous screens: I prefer to see the whole shape of the hymn before me, so that I can see how it builds to a climax.

7. For suggestions as to what the "better" might consist of see Bradbury, "Sticky Faith," 22–25.

loss is one of the measures of our poverty, and the primary secret
of inefficient life and service.[8]

Extricating myself from the hymnological quagmire, I turn to the
prayers in worship. The question whether prayers should be free/conceived
or read has sometimes been a bone of contention in our churches. Among
the Separatist harbingers of Congregationalism the pattern was set early.
In 1588 a deposition was lodged against a church comprising those who
followed Henry Barrow. It contains a description of the church's worship
which includes the following observation: "In their praier one speketh and
the rest doe groan, or sob, or sigh, as if they would ring out teares . . . there
prayer is extemporal. In there conventicles they use not the lordes praier,
not any forme of sett praier."[9] Lying behind this stance is the determination
not to be bound by the words of men, especially when those words have
been prescribed by the monarch and parliament, who had no right to order
the worship of the church which, in spiritual matters, was solely accountable to Christ its Head (though it is surprising that their biblicism did not
permit them to use the very words Jesus had given his disciples). Above all
they believed that the Holy Spirit would give them the words they needed.

During the eighteenth century the question of free versus set prayers
was zealously debated in some Presbyterian circles. Samuel Bourn, for example sought to strike a balance thus:

> I shou'd rather choose to join a Society where the work of publick
> Prayer is carried on by the free use of a Man's Talents, who is well
> qualified for his office . . . than with a Society who are content with
> Prayers pre-composed, which cannot fit all Cases either of the So-
> ciety in general, or of its particular Members, and which must grow
> dry and tasteless by frequent Repetitions. On the other hand, were
> all other Circumstances equal, I think I shou'd choose stately to join
> with a Society where pre-composed Forms . . . are used, which are
> proper, grave, methodical, apt and moving, and are seriously offered
> up to God, than with a Society, where a Man is stately employ'd,
> who fills his Prayers with fantastical, conceited Expressions, private
> Notions, senseless Sounds, tedious babblings, and affected Heats.[10]

When some Presbyterian ministers in Liverpool let it be known that they
intended to introduce set prayers, their colleague John Taylor took up his

8. Quoted by Porritt, *John Henry Jowett*, 97.

9. Burrage, *Early English Dissenters*, II, 27.

10. Bourn, *The Young Christian's Prayer Book*, viii.

pen against them in *The Scripture Account of Prayer*. While he expected free prayer to be rational, he maintained that reading prayers would bring no esteem to a minister, for in Dissenting congregations "it is considered a very low manner of performing the office."[11] He further argued that "People pray as they believe,"[12] and that those who use a set liturgy are credally constricted, and tempted to utter what they do not believe.

It must be admitted that some of the opposition to read prayers flowed from the view that because the Church of England required it, it must be wrong! As late as the early years of my ministry this attitude prevailed in some quarters. Indeed, I remember being "muttered against" on one occasion by one who disapprovingly confided to her friend, "I think he read that prayer." I had indeed done so, and was sorely tempted thereafter (truth to tell, I occasionally yielded) to tease the saints by praying freely in collect form. Not the least formative influence upon me in the matter of public prayer was the exemplary skill of Principal W. Gordon Robinson in the art and craft of free prayer. He was not opposed to read prayers (nor am I), but he did believe that free/conceived prayer was becoming increasingly at risk as service books became more generally available and used (as do I). Thus while he chaired the committee that produced *A Book of Services and Prayers* (1959)[13] for The Congregational Union of England and Wales—a book which contains both orders of worship in which extensive but not exclusive space is given to free prayer and "A Treasury of Prayers from Ancient Liturgies" and from "Reformers and Congregationalists"—he also published anonymously *Our Heritage of Free Prayer*, in which he included much practical guidance for those seeking to master the art and craft. I

11. Taylor, *The Scripture Account of Prayer*, 5.

12. Ibid., 71.

13. Tony Tucker describes this book as to a degree representing "the apogee of the Genevan liturgical tradition within English Congregationalism." See *Reformed Ministry*, 125. In this context "Genevan" refers to those ministers and laypersons who sought to recover aspects of the Reformed heritage for Congregationalism at large. They formed the Church Order Group for this purpose. It is sometimes thought that alumni of Mansfield College were solely responsible for this development. It should be noted (a) that ministers educated elsewhere—including a significant number from Yorkshire United Independent College—were members of the Church Order Group; and (b) that eight of the thirteen members of the committee that devised *A Book of Services and Prayers* were not Mansfield alumni (the committee secretary, H. F. Leatherland, among them), and some of them were decidedly not "Genevans". For their names, see the *Book*, vii. In my opinion, the book represented a healthy balance of the several tendencies within Congregationalist worship of the period.

need only add that in six years of his own prayers in the college chapel, which were variously prompted by the seasons of the Christian Year, the Bible passages read, the prevailing circumstances of the times, he was ever fresh, and could not have been less repetitive. He devoted much care to his prayers (but was not so lost in them as not to notice who had turned up to chapel in carpet slippers).

It remains only to add that ministers should pay heed to the several parts of prayer, some of which I specified in the skeletal order of worship set out above. After conducting a service on one occasion I was staggered to be thanked for my prayer of confession, because "It is such a long time since we had one of those." That observation is indicative of more than a liturgical failure, it is a pastoral failure, in that since all of us are sinners as well as saints, to omit the prayer of confession is to deprive the worshippers of an opportunity to confess their sins, hear the assurance of God's pardon, and go on their way assured of God's forgiving love in Christ and empowered by the Holy Spirit to live a renewed life. In this sense confession and good news are inextricably interwoven, and it is tragic if people leave the church feeling as guilty as they did when they entered it. On the other hand, there are also prayers of confession which have the effect of unwarrantably heaping upon worshippers guilt in respect of matters over which they have no control, and for which they are not morally responsible. I well remember the woman who said to me, during the height of the anti-apartheid crusade in South Africa, "Our minister is such a nice young man, but in his prayers of confession he will keep making me feel that everything that goes wrong in South Africa is my fault." This way lies liturgical unreality. More than that, it scuppers morality, for we cannot be objectively morally responsible for the misdeeds of others (though we would be morally responsible for words and/or actions which influenced those concerned—positively by tempting them, or negatively by not seeking to dissuade them). As for the sinful acts of our forebears: while we may regret, even deplore them, and resolve with God's help not to repeat them, we did not actually commit them: we simply were not there, and hence cannot be held morally responsible for them. Above all, it is bad theology, for it turns God into one who randomly dispenses feelings of guilt, without regard to personal intentions, circumstances, or moral culpability.

Where the parts of prayer are concerned, Isaac Watts put most of what is necessary in four crisp lines:

> Call upon God, adore, confess,

> Petition, plead, and then declare
> You are the Lord's, give thanks and bless,
> And let Amen confirm the prayer.[14]

I need hardly add that where free/conceived prayer is concerned, there is a relationship between what comes out of the mouth and what has previously gone in by way of meditation, prayer, Bible study, and pastoral experience among those whose prayers the minister is privileged to offer in public worship. It goes without saying that the entire preparation and delivery is undertaken in reliance upon the guidance and stimulation of God the Holy Spirit.

Since the ministry of the Word is central in the service, one would expect that readings from the Bible would always be present. I recall, however, the Order of Worship of a church to which I was sent to preach whilst a student, which included the following item: "Reading from the Bible or other suitable literature." I thought then, and I think now, that no literature is suitable as an alternative to, or replacement of, the Bible, for God addresses us by the Spirit through the Scriptures within the fellowship. Moreover, we listen to it together. That is to say, I believe that hearing God's word in public worship is a corporate act, and that it is to some extent diminished if people follow the readings in their own Bibles. This can appear as a lapse into individualism (compare the Catholic who goes to church to "make *my* communion"), though if people find it helpful to follow the words for themselves I shall not go to the stake on the issue.[15]

I find that the lectionary is increasingly used in our churches, and, given the fidelity of those leading the worship to the prescribed passages, this can prompt us to recall that in many churches Christians are pursuing kindred themes. It may also dissuade some preachers from fastening on their favourite texts, though I have not infrequently found that some preachers are not above proceeding with their "travelling mercies" despite the lectionary. Again, whether a lectionary is in use or not (and we are not bound to use a lectionary), there is much to be said for following the tradition of reading from the Old Testament, the Epistles, and the Gospels; and it can be easier to make three freely selected readings feed into the sermon than to wrestle some lectionary selections into coherence with it. This is

---

14. Watts, *A Guide to Prayer*, 50.

15. From among the many available versions of the Bible, I find that *The Revised English Bible* and *The New Revised Standard Version* of the Bible are most suitable in terms of accuracy and readability whether audible or silent.

not surprising, since lectionary readings are designed to be read, as it were, horizontally across a period of weeks, and there is no expectation that the readings for any given Sunday will necessarily converge upon a common theme. I have noticed that on occasion even those who are most ardently in favour of the lectionary will take refuge in Christian Aid Sunday, or Prisons Sunday, or some similar occasion, and will avoid any reference to the readings of the day.

The reading of the Bible in public worship is of very great importance, and it needs to be done audibly and intelligently. Whether or not the lectionary is used, I believe that even (and sometimes especially) familiar Bible passages should be rehearsed by those appointed read them. Hearers are not helped when the wrong words are emphasized, or when the sense is submerged under gabbling; and I have lost count of how many times I have been informed that Mary and Joseph and the baby were, by the neglect of comma and the omission of a slight pause, all in the manger together (Luke 2:16).

In some Reformed churches, following the order of the injunction of Psalm 96:8 (cf. 1 Chr 16:29), "Bring an offering, and come into his courts," money is contributed by the worshippers at the door of the church on their way in. I think it better to regard the offertory as part of the saints' response to the gospel. It stands for the consecration of their material goods to the service of God. It is that more than a collection to keep the organization in being and, with a view to avoiding that interpretation, it is best separated from the announcements. It is a corporate act of gratitude to God for all his goodness to us. Our thoughts should be along the lines of George Herbert's words in his 1633 poem "Gratefulnesse":

> Thou that hast giv'n so much to me,
> Give one thing more, a gratefull heart.

Conversely, if people do not believe that God has in Christ done something remarkable for them, their motivation to give will be correspondingly weak. Grateful people give, and if people are unaware of what has been done for them, the answer lies more in the proclamation of the gospel than in gift day appeal letters, no matter how elegantly and tactfully they are phrased.

Clearly, the offering is too important to be camouflaged by a hymn. It is a significant act of worship in its own right, and it should be conducted with reverence, and not as it was by an oleaginous minister of a large church who sent round plastic buckets for the receipt of what he called a "silent offering"—by which he meant that only what Arthur Daley[16] (of whom he was also in other ways reminiscent) would have understood as "folding money" would do.

We come next in the service to the Lord's Supper. I do not, of course, deny that the sacrament is a Eucharist (thanksgiving) or a Holy Communion (though it is more than a "breaking of bread"), but this is my preferred, and our traditional, name for the sacrament. It was used by Paul (1 Cor 11:20), and it clearly marks the distinction between the Last Supper of the first Maundy Thursday and the post-Easter Lord's Supper. The events of the Last Supper are recalled, but the sacrament is set in the context of the victory of the Cross and its Easter confirmation. The context is quite different, hence the alternative name of the sacrament, Eucharist.

In the previous chapter I outlined the meaning of the sacrament, but now I am thinking of how it is conducted in the service. The United Reformed Church, like its predecessor traditions, believes that at the Supper the risen Christ is the host, and that all who by grace are called by the Holy Spirit under the preaching of the gospel, and engrafted into Christ as branches of the Vine, are necessarily related to all the other branches (John 15:5). Hence the Lord's table is open to all who are his. In this we witness to our catholicity. When we profess our faith and are received as members of the church we are indeed, as it were, locally anchored saints, but we are at the same time members of the church catholic, of which the local church is an expression. It is tragic that the one church of Christ is divided at his table, and it is an important part of our practice that in this respect at least we are not sectarian. As long ago as 1839, at the first Autumn Assembly of the Congregational Union of England and Wales, my distinguished predecessor at Angel Street, Worcester, George Redford, declared it to be an example of Congregationalism's catholicity that "we can admit Christians of all denominations to our communion."[17] In this he took his cue from the Gospels, and cited the universality of the Saviour. If the Fourth Gospel gives us Jesus as the Vine and ourselves as the branches, John Calvin, turning to the epistles, appeals to the equally corporate image of the body and its limbs (1 Cor 12:12–27), and affirms that "The church is called 'catholic', or 'universal', because there could not be two or three churches unless Christ

---

16. A prominent character (memorably played by George Cole), in the British television series *Minder*, who was a tradesman given to "dodgy" schemes that seldom, if ever, met his expectations.

17. Quoted by A. Peel, *These Hundred Years*, 111.

be torn asunder—which cannot happen! But all the elect are so united in Christ that as they are dependent on one Head, they also grow together in one body, being joined and knit together as the limbs of a body."[18]

Three points remain to be noted. First, it was a longstanding custom in many of our churches that after the hymn following the sermon and a grace (in other words, at the end of the liturgy of the catechumens), those who had not made their profession of faith would withdraw, the minister greeting them at the door, and the Lord's Supper, sometimes called the "second service" (classically, the liturgy of the faithful), would then take place. With the increasing acceptance of the order of worship I am following in this chapter, which brings Word and sacrament together, the older practice has been discarded in many churches. It did, however, make the point that the sacrament is a sacrament of the church, and this point can be lost as things now stand, not least when children (baptized or not) are invited to take communion. I am not suggesting that the Lord's Supper should, as it were, be hidden away from people until they understand the full significance of it, (a) because none of us ever attains to such a position; and (b) because I think it well that children are present at the sacrament, for they can be moved by the sense of reverence and awe, and because a measure of understanding is more likely to follow if they have been within eye-and-earshot of the service than if they have not. But the Lord's Supper remains a sacrament of the church and the church comprises believers. For these reasons we have to take care that we do not prevent members of any Christian tradition from coming to the table, but we also have to follow up pastorally those who may come but have not fulfilled their baptism, professed their faith and become enrolled saints.

Secondly, by long tradition, baptized children of the covenant would, often from the age of sixteen upwards, confess their faith, be received or admitted as members of the church, and be inducted into the responsibilities of "full" membership of the church. In the Congregational tradition the promises they were invited to make were of almost monastic rigour. The following is among the three questions asked in the last major service book of the Congregational Union of England and Wales:

> Do you promise to obey God's holy will, and to walk according to his commandments all the days of your life? Do you resolve to fulfil the duties of membership in the Church, joining regularly in public worship, in the Communion of the Lord's Supper, and in

18. Calvin, *Institutes of the Christian Religion*, IV.i.2.

the Church Meeting; and, being faithful in Bible reading and in prayer, in giving and in service?[19]

The Confirmation Services which have been published by The United Reformed Church since 1972 are less specific. The following typifies the kind of promise sought: "Do you promise, trusting in God's grace, to be faithful in public and private worship, to live in the fellowship of the Church, to share in its witness?"[20]

I regret the lack of specificity, not least because I believe that especially at a time of overall membership decline nothing is gained by reducing the challenge of church membership (or by lowering the standards for entry to the ministry of the gospel, for that matter). May it be that the lack of specificity relates in part to the fact that persons are confirmed at a younger age than hitherto—even as young as twelve, especially in some Local Ecumenical Partnerships? I concede that attendance at Church Meeting, for example, may not be the favourite pastime of a twelve-year-old. This is why I think it important that as confirmed young people reach adulthood instruction in our heritage and polity be given to them so that they can fully grasp what the responsibilities of adult church membership within and beyond the local church are. They could even reaffirm their commitment at the Lord's table. Such help and encouragement might well encourage some who were received/confirmed in their early teenage years to become responsible adult members of the church. If young adults—and, indeed, older ones too—seek confirmation/membership within a Local Ecumenical Partnership, I think it well that they become acquainted with the principles and order of the traditions which comprise the Partnership, so that they may understand how and why their churchly life is ordered as it is.

Thirdly, concerns of a different order are sometimes expressed regarding the bread and wine used at the Lord's Supper. As to the bread, I think it more important that communicants who need gluten free bread are accommodated than that we become liturgically precious concerning the "one loaf." A similar attitude should be taken to those who on principle or for health reasons wish to drink unfermented wine. In neither case is it difficult to make the necessary arrangements. What, then of the common cup, and the derision sometimes poured upon individual communion glasses (whose original manufacturers undeniably played the health card in marketing them)? I understand the theology of the common cup, though

19. *A Book of Services and Prayers*, 55.

20. *Service Book*, 42.

in a large congregation, as soon as more than one chalice is used the logic is undone and one might as well have numerous individual cups. When communicants proceed to the Lord's table in groups to receive the chalice the idea of all eating and drinking together, which is preserved when the bread and wine in individual glasses are received by the people in their seats, is lost. I do not think that any of these ways and means should cause distress or lead to dissension. The primary objective should be the reverent keeping of the Supper, and in this respect my preference is for keeping music and choirs at bay for the duration: there is not too much silence in our worship. However, since I know that some find appropriate musical accompaniment helpful, a half-and-half compromise would not, I think, delay the *parousia*.

The blessing is the climax of the service. A number of biblical blessings may be used, but in my view the blessing in the name of the holy Trinity is of supreme importance.[21] At all events, the blessing is not a prayer, nor is it a humanistic dismissal of the flock. Here, as in preaching, the minister stands before the people as Christ's representative, and in the name of God the saints are blessed and despatched near and far to make their witness and offer their service in the world. Professor T. F. Torrance, newly ordained, expressed to his father his uncertainty as to his role. His father replied, "You are ordained to bless the people in the name of God."[22] Could there be any higher calling?

Having progressed through the bare bones of the order of the Service of Word and Sacrament it might seem that we are ready for the next chapter on the minister of the gospel's specific duties of preaching and pastoral care. But first there is one more very important occasion of worship to be noted. I refer to the Church Meeting. Of our three councils: Church Meeting, Synod and General Assembly, Church Meeting is probably the most misunderstood, not least within our own ranks. I do not think my ears deceived me when, as I followed a staunch church member up the path to Church Meeting, I heard him say to a newly received member, "You'll enjoy Church Meeting: it's where we all stick our oar in!" It would seem that it was ever thus. The scholarly minister of Hampstead Congregational Church, R. F. Horton, lamented that his church members did "not know what a Church Meeting is. In fifty years I have failed to teach them."[23] More recently David

21. See further Appendix I below.

22. Quoted by Iain R. Torrance, "Thomas F. Torrance's Theology of Ministry and the Pressing Issues of Today," 522.

23. A. Peel and Marriott, *Robert Forman Horton*, 186.

Peel has observed, with regret, that "we lost sight of the primary purpose of the Church Meeting long ago."[24] I deliberately referred to Church Meeting as an occasion of worship. It is a continuation of Sunday worship. It is a credal assembly where, as on Sundays, we confess the Lordship of Christ, and we bring it all down to earth, so to speak, by asking, "What are we to do with this gospel that we have heard in the preaching and seen enacted at the Lord's Supper? How are we to witness to it in the place where God has set us? How are we to serve our immediate community, and how, through our prayers and gifts, are we to sustain the wider ministries of the church, and play our part in the socio-political affairs of the day?

All of this might be described as outward-looking worship. But Church Meeting is concerned with more particular matters too. Traditionally the names of those to be received as members have been brought before the Meeting. Indeed, in earlier times such persons would have been invited to the Meeting to testify to the work of God in their lives. Later, the minister, or a deacon or elder could speak on their behalf, and today names are referred to Church Meeting by the Elders' Meeting, and this is as it should be. I believe that the same should happen in relation to those seeking believer baptism, and those whose parents seek infant baptism for their children. In these cases it matters to the church who is to be received, and in baptism services the local church promises to receive the person baptized and to surround them with such nurture and care as are appropriate. It has always seemed to me odd if the first time the members hear of the baptismal candidate is at the baptism service itself. Rather, when names have been brought to Church Meeting the pastoral concern for the family should immediately begin to be expressed, and that not only in the person of the minister. Baptism is primarily a churchly, not a domestic or a social, occasion. If those to be baptized are not children of the covenant, their parents should be instructed in the faith in the hope that they will be received as members on the day their child is baptized. Sometimes we too glibly speak of requests for infant baptism by those who are not church members as providing us with evangelical opportunities. But if that is what they are, how assiduously do we pursue them? I have never heard of a case in which parents were received as church members for the first time, and their child was baptized, at one and the same service.[25]

24. D. R. Peel, *Ministry for Mission*, 50.

25. Presumably in order to make a gesture towards the idea that the sacraments are sacraments of the church, John Conder of Homerton College advised his students thus:

Lastly, I would mention the question of church discipline. Our old church books burst with examples of those who were disciplined for falling asleep during the sermon, consorting with somebody else's wife, giving themselves to malicious gossip, and much else besides. It is not impossible that some enjoyed the "policing of the saints" rather too much, but, happily, there is reason to think that Richard Baxter's "softly-softly" approach was not untypical:

> I do, if it be secret, make the fault at first no more public than the owner made it, but secretly admonish him to repent and reform. If it be public, or if he repent not, and reform not, I admonish before two or three, and then call him to our meeting . . . and there endeavour his humiliation and reformation. If he declare not repentance there, or if he do but return again to the sin, I do in the face of the congregation mention his crime, and our proceedings, and again with all seriousness and compassion there summon him to repentance: and if he refuse I desire the congregation to join in earnest prayer for him. This I do once or twice or thrice as prudence shall direct, considering the quality of the sin and sinner and the measure of the scandal. If yet he hear not the church, I do, from certain texts recited, require them to avoid him . . .[26]

Properly understood, church discipline was intended to serve four purposes: to glorify God, to uphold the integrity of the church, to ensure that the weaker brothers and sister would not be harmed and to caution all, and to restore repentant offenders. All of this was derived from the conviction that the church was in a proper sense, separated from the (ungodly) world, and separated unto the Lord. In other words, it was to be a holy people, disciplined for its work and witness in the (geographical) world. As I wrote thirty years ago, "How preposterous to suppose that these objectives could be secured in a loveless manner!"[27]

I am well aware that to some, even within The United Reformed Church, the idea of the church as comprising the saints, separated unto the Lord, is understood as a hard saying, for "inclusiveness" is their watchword. It goes without saying that the welcoming of people of all sorts and conditions is an aspect of the church's mission. But the commendation of Christ as Saviour and Lord, and the prayerful hope that others will find new life

---

"Baptize the Children of those who are not Members privately and not in the Church—which cases you will find much the most numerous." See his "Divinity Lectures," 533.

26. Dr. Williams's Library, London, MS 2: 256.

27. Sell, *Guidelines on Church Discipline*, 13.

in him are also aspects of that same mission. To be in Christ is to be of the church, it is to be a visible saint. To put it otherwise, the church comprises Christians. We may not behave as if Jews, Muslims, Hindus, atheists and others, all of whom we may be called upon to befriend and serve, are simply waiting to be annexed by us. Furthermore, as P. Mark Achtemeier has rightly said, "The 'inclusiveness' of the mainline Protestant churches is now in danger of becoming a completely elastic concept, embracing and affirming every private and idiosyncratic belief system, regardless of whether it stands in any discernible continuity with historic Christianity, much less Reformed faith."[28] Is it conceivable that nowadays we have become so identified with the surrounding culture as to be almost indistinguishable from it? If this is the case it is no surprise either that we find it difficult to witness to those around us, or that it does not occur to our neighbours that we might have anything distinctive, or of importance, to say to them.

28. Achtemeier, "The *Union with Christ* Doctrine in Renewal Movements of the Presbyterian Church (USA)," 343.

# 4

# The Work of the Ministry
## (2) Preaching and Pastoral Care

HOWEVER THE GIFTS OF a minister of the gospel are to be shared among the churches at the present time (on which subject I shall have more to say in the following chapter), the proclamation of the good news and the care of the flock are, and must remain, central to that work. The church was created by the gospel. The good news of God's love and mercy supremely revealed, active and victorious at the Cross was proclaimed and, by the gracious call of God the Holy Spirit, those who made a response of faith—itself a gift of the Spirit so that none should boast (Eph 2:9)—the church was gathered. Whereas much of the service which the church offers to society in terms of peacemaking, the quest of justice, feeding the hungry, and much else besides, can be undertaken by those who do not perform it in Christ's name, the proclamation of the gospel that created it is the church's distinctive task, and if the church fails here, nobody else will pick up the torch.

## THE PREACHER'S AUTHORITY

What a diversity of preachers the church has spawned—and in some cases suffered. In the course of a paper read to the members of the international Reformed-Methodist dialogue commission I presumed to liken the Methodists to ourselves in a variety of ways, among them the following: "We have had pulpit giants and pulpit autocrats; we have had lay preachers whose proudest boast was that they had not sat under any theological professor but they had sat at the feet of Christ; we have had ministers whose sermons have given little evidence that they had sat in either place."[1] These examples suggest the wisdom of taking our bearings from elsewhere. What is the preacher's task?

In the context of public worship it is the minister's high privilege and great challenge to stand for Christ before the people and rehearse the good news that is the very lifeblood of the church and of every individual saint. As John Owen put it, "The first great duty of the ministry, with reference unto the church, is the dispensation of the gospel unto it, for its edification. . . . [I]t is the principal work of the ministry, the foundation of all other duties, which the apostles themselves gave themselves unto in an especial manner" (Acts 4:4).[2] Ministers do not act in this way on their own authority, or because of their training or oratorical gifts. Their authority derives from the Lord who is himself the good news. This was the point that Paul emphasized to the Corinthians who were questioning his authority. He greeted them as "Paul, apostle of Christ Jesus by God's call and by his will" (1 Cor 1: 1); and when writing to the Romans he was more specific, describing himself as "Paul, servant of Christ Jesus, called by God to be an apostle and set apart for the service of his gospel" (Rom 1:1). Our ministers are similarly called, and they stand in the succession of those who preach the apostles' gospel. They are commissioned ambassadors of Christ, and what they proclaim is not a message of their own concocting, and it is not their possession. Still less is it given to them by the church in which they are ordained. Hear this from Bernard Manning's ordination charge:

> Do not . . . flatter yourselves. . . . The things that make a man a good minister of Jesus Christ come from God most high: you can neither bestow them nor take them away. . . . At your hands indeed he receives the commission; but it is Christ's commission, not yours; and it comes from Christ, not you. When your minister speaks, mark whose word it is that he speaks. You do not hear

---

1. Sell, *Dissenting Thought and the Life of the* Churches, 607. A. J. Grieve reminded any who were disposed to repudiate theology that in his teaching Jesus constantly challenged his hearers to the theological task of rethinking their ideas of God: "many a deacon and many evangelist who has expressed [the dismissive] sentiment or left it unexpressed is now busily engaged in trying to explain himself in heaven." See "Christian Learning and Christian Living," 71.

2. Owen, *Works*, IV, 508.

from him an echo of your own voice. It is the Word of God that
He proclaims, no word that you have committed to him tonight.[3]

The gospel is God's founding gift to the church; the message belongs to all the saints, and it is to be heralded by all through their several ministries. But the minister has the awesome task of regularly and publicly articulating it—a task made none the less weighty by the realization that the minister himself is a sinner in no less need of God's forgiving grace than any of the saints. Is there any preacher who has not felt as Jeremiah did when God called him to be a prophet: "Ah! Lord God . . . I am not skilled in speaking, I am too young"? (Jer 1:6). But God sent him on his mission with the assurance that he would be given what he had to say. So it is with Christian ministers who are charged with proclaiming the message of salvation and calling on their peers to repent, believe, and receive new life in Christ. In the absence of divine aid ministers could not even begin the task. Thomas Watson never wrote more truly than when he declared that "The ministers of God are only the pipes and organs; it is the Spirit blowing in them that effectually changes the heart."[4]

All of which is to say that when the gospel is preached something special is taking place. We are not listening to someone airing his or her knowledge, or presenting a lecture, or letting loose bees in his or her bonnet, or off-loading his or her latest thoughts on this or that. When the gospel is proclaimed we are listening to the word that God has given his minister for us. It is a word that the minister has received through concentrated Bible study and ardent prayer, and the minister speaks in reliance upon the Holy Spirit who will bring God's word home to the people. Lovell Cocks, ever to the point, observed that "When we are commissioned to preach we are commanded to do what can never be done by men. . . . To preach and hear the Word of God does not stand in our power as sinful men. . . . The Holy Spirit is the only preacher."[5] This is a high view of preaching, and it is ours. It is as far from downloading a sermon from the internet at 22.00 on a Saturday evening as it could possibly be.

Traditionally, the sermon has been delivered from a pulpit, for this was the place where this special activity took place. Today, however, I notice that some ministers seem to shun the pulpit. This is understandable if the building has one or two galleries, the pulpit is very high, and the people are

3. Manning, *A Layman in the Ministry*, 153.

4. Watson, *A Divine Cordial*, 78.

5. Cocks, "The Place of the Sermon in Worship," 268.

scattered around the ground floor. But even then there can be a designated site for this special activity. Regardless of the shape of the building some ministers prefer to pace about on a dais, sometimes speaking off the back of an envelope, and I understand that they do this either because they do not, as they put it, wish to be "six feet above criticism"—a fatuous excuse which shows a complete lack of understanding of their high calling—or because they think that this enables them to get close to the people in a friendly kind of way. (The latter are frequently the same ones whose "call to worship" is "Good morning everybody"). It is puzzling, but I have also noticed that some of those who are so eager to get close to the people on Sundays are the very ones who seem to hide from them for the rest of the week.[6]

## FEEDING THE FLOCK

I mentioned God's call to Jeremiah, and in the biblical book which bears his name there is much food for thought where preaching is concerned. As with Amos, so with Jeremiah: God is the Lord of nature and of nations; as with Hosea, he is the God of love and righteousness who longs to woo his wayward people back home; like Micah, Jeremiah understands that God's presence is not confined to the temple; on the contrary, God approaches people in the most intimate way, writing a new covenant not on tablets of stone, but on their hearts. All of these notes are sounded in turbulent times. As if the threat of powerful neighbours were not enough, the government of Zedekiah, the last king of Judah, is weak and ineffectual. He is quite unable to control the chieftains of the people, whom the prophet lambasts as false shepherds who lead the flock astray, scatter it, and fail to feed it.

These false shepherds will not, however, have the last word. Another of Jeremiah's characteristics is his underlying hopefulness and confidence in God. He reports God as saying that he will gather the remnant of his scattered flock; he will appoint shepherds who will feed them. More than that, a sprout or shoot (coded messianic talk here) shall spring up who will rule wisely and execute justice in the land. In Ezekiel 34 we have similar denunciations of false shepherds, and the same commitment on God's part to search for his sheep himself, and to "feed them on good grazing-ground" (Ezek 34:14). To this Deutero Isaiah (Isaiah 40–55) adds the messianic

---

6. One of my friends has suggested that in this paragraph I betray irritation. What I hope to convey is disappointment—even astonishment—that the high calling of preaching can be so sadly misunderstood.

emphasis. Whoever he thought the coming servant of the Lord would be, he prophesied that he would "feed his flock like a shepherd." As Christians know, Jesus thought of himself in terms of the good shepherd who, unlike the false hireling shepherds, lays down his life for the sheep (John 10:1–18), and feeds us on the bread of life, which nourishes us for life eternal. It is the good news of this shepherd that ministerial under-shepherds are to proclaim. This is why, in a sermon delivered to the vacant pastorate of Milton Church, Glasgow, on 1 November 1840, John "Rabbi" Duncan exhorted his hearers, as they sought their next minister, to "Look for the man who appears most to have seen, most to be beholding, the Lamb of God, and whose whole address points you away from himself and all others to behold the Lamb of God."[7]

Those who preach at Horton-in-Craven Congregational Church (1816) can hardly fail to be challenged as to their role. For as they stand in the pulpit and look straight ahead they see, at eye level, the front of a small gallery on which the following words are inscribed:

> Let no base hireling here intrude
> To feed the flock with poisonous food.
> Kind Shepherd for Thy flock prepare
> Pure living streams and pastures fair.
> Come in ye thirsty, don't delay,
> Drink wine and milk from day to day;
> Sweet Jesus calls you come away,
> Flee now to Him this very day.

How effectively are we feeding Christ's flock? With what are we feeding them? Do the hungry sheep, today as of old, look up and find that they are not being fed?[8]

Before coming to matters concerning the preparation and content of sermons, it will be worthwhile to ponder the preacher's attitude towards preaching, for this will influence both the content used and the objectives sought. "How should ministers preach?" asked William Bagshawe, the Presbyterian who became known as "the Apostle of the Peak." He answered his question with a series of adverbs: "Compassionately, plainly, experimentally, clearly, zealously, faithfully, solidly, wisely, distinguishingly,

---

7. Duncan, *Pulpit and Communion Table*, 230.

8. The allusion here is to John Milton's poem "Lycidas," line 125.

takingly, Scripturally, longingly after the conversion of the hearers."[9] All of these are to the point, but I wish to focus upon three more adverbs which are, I believe, of particular relevance at the present time: urgently, honestly, and expectantly.

First, preaching should be imbued with a sense of urgency. If we do not think it matters whether or not people hear and receive the gospel, our preaching is doomed: in fact, it is a sham. As the Scottish divine, D. W. Forrest put it, "'To-day, if ye will hear His voice', is the note which the preacher must ever sound, if he is to keep man's responsibility at its true height and rightly present the urgency of his Divine message."[10] The sense of urgency, not to mention the eschatological consequences of his preaching, struck Robert Murray M'Cheyne with even greater force:

> As I was walking in the fields, the thought came over me with almost overwhelming power, that every one of my flock must soon be in heaven or hell. Oh how I wished that I had a tongue like thunder, that I make all hear; or that I had a frame like iron, that I might visit every one, and say, "Escape for thy life!" Ah, sinners! you little know how I fear that you will lay the blame of your damnation at my door."[11]

If ever we are tempted to make light of sin, or if like a correspondent to *Reform* we cannot think of ourselves as sinners (the first one is pride!), we need to take with due seriousness what it cost God at the Cross to deal with it. If we are ever tempted to rejoice in humanity's ever-upward progress, and to follow an older theological liberalism in thinking of hell as "frozen over or turned to innocuous ashes,"[12] M'Cheyne will at least remind us of the gospel challenge to determine whether we are for God or Mammon; he may even remind us of the biblical principle upon which the polity of The United Reformed Church turns, namely, that there is a distinction of eternal significance between those who are in Christ and those who are opposed to him. Not, indeed, that it is for us to predict what any person's eternal destination will be. But while we earnestly proclaim God's ever-seeking love, we should also be aware that nothing erodes the urgency of preaching more swiftly than a glib universalism which presumes to predict happy landings for all—as if the sin on account of which Jesus suffered on

9. Quoted by Brentall, *William Bagshawe*, 85.

10. Leckie, *David W. Forrest, DD*, 126.

11. Bonar, *The Life of Robert Murray M'Cheyne*, 172.

12. Quoted by Horsch, *Modern Religious Liberalism*, 127–28.

the Cross, or the dreadful agonies which flow from the actions of today's tyrants, were of no account. As Spurgeon observed in his homely way, "If, for a moment, our improvements seem to produce a larger result than the old gospel, it will be the growth of mushrooms, it may even be the growth of toadstools; but it is not the growth of trees of the Lord."[13] Not for nothing did Richard Baxter quite regularly think of himself as preaching "as a dying man to dying men."[14]

Secondly, the preacher should be honest in preaching. The redoubtable John Knox is famed for having bluntly told Queen Mary, "I am in the place where I am demanded of conscience to speak the truth. . . . The truth I speak, impugn it whoso list."[15] There is no doubt that Knox would have approved of John Bunyan's attitude, "I preached what I felt, what I smartingly did feel."[16] Knox and Bunyan remind us that to be honest in preaching is more than telling the truth and refraining from telling lies. For in preaching we are testifying to what we have seen and heard. Personal integrity, not simply making true statements and shunning false ones, is at stake here. Hence James Denney's cautionary word:

> The preacher's peril is the peril of coming to men in word only; saying things which he does not feel . . . uttering truths, it may be, but truths which have never done anything for him—enlightened, quickened, or sanctified him—and which he cannot hope, as they come from his lips, will do anything for others; or worse still, uttering things of which he cannot even be confident that they are true.[17]

How relieved the evangelical Anglican William Romaine was when he was able to say, "I have the peace of God in my conscience. . . . I knew before that the doctrines I preached were truths, but now I experience them to be blessings."[18] If I have failed to make my point sufficiently clearly, Spurgeon will again come to my aid: "We may not be butchers at the block chopping off for hungry ones meat of which we do not partake."[19] Honesty is frequently called for in the details of a sermon. A minister would be dishonest

13. Spurgeon, *An All-Round Ministry*, 376.

14. Baxter, *Poetical Fragments*, 40.

15. Knox, *The History of the Reformation in Scotland*, 297.

16. Bunyan, *Grace Abounding to the Chief of Sinners*, 70.

17. Denney, *The Epistles to the Thessalonians*, 48–9.

18. Romaine, *Letters from the late Rev. William Romaine, M.A. . . . to a Friend*, 207.

19. Spurgeon, *An All-round Ministry*, 66.

if he spoke as if Adam were an historical character whilst believing that he was not. But if the point of referring to Adam is to expound sin as being that human rebellion against God which says, "We will not have you to reign over us," there is no need to encourage the saints into off-the-point speculations regarding the historicity of Adam, still less the theological meaning of "myth." These latter topics are not unimportant but, as we shall see in the next chapter, they are best treated in Bible study meetings.

Thirdly, ministers are to preach expectantly. It is said that "a certain unhappy divinity student stood before his college principal, who had in front of him the student's latest and best sermon. There was a frosty silence as they eyed one another. At length the student burst out, 'It *will* do, sir, won't it?' The principal's acid reply was, 'It will do *what*?'"[20] Ministers should preach expectantly not, indeed, because they think that by their oratory they will arouse the multitude or prod the remnant, but because they know that when the gospel is faithfully preached, however humbly and falteringly, it is followed by the Holy Spirit's blessing. Indeed, by the illuminating work of the Holy Spirit the word preached is heard and received as God's Word, and that Word cannot fail to bear some fruit. Calvin held that the preaching of the Word and the sacraments "can never exist without bringing forth fruit and prospering by God's blessing." He immediately allows that the fruit may not appear immediately, but "wherever it is received and has a fixed abode, it shows its effectiveness."[21] Do ministers really expect that anything of any consequence will result from their preaching? It is not possible to say how much the Revd William Haslam of Baldhu, Truro, expected from his 1851 sermon on the text, "What think ye of Christ?" (Matt 22:42). In the course of his exposition he began to see in Christ what the Pharisees did not, and a change came over his appearance and delivery, so that a lay preacher in the congregation stood up and declared "The parson is converted! Hallelujah!" Whereupon the people burst forth in praise.[22]

It may be that genuine modesty on the part of a minister dampens the expectation of great things. To those who might feel that they cannot emulate Paul, F. W. Bourne pointed out that

> You have the same Gospel to preach, the same cross in which to glory, the same gate of eternal life to open, as he had. You may be filled by the same power, cheered by the same presence, sustained

20. Davies, "The Minister as Preacher and Teacher," 123.

21. Calvin, *Institutes*, IV.i.10.

22. For Haslam's account of his conversion see *From Death into Life*, ch. 7.

by the same promises, as he was. You bear in your hands the same cup of healing, filled with the precious balm of Gilead, for the recovery of diseased souls; you carry the same message of mercy and salvation to lost souls, and you invite poor sinners to the same Saviour and heaven, as he did. There is no reason, therefore, why you should not "always triumph in Christ," and rejoice in buds of promise and fruits of righteousness on every hand. . . . You are to make Christ's name radiant with glory, fill his cup with joys, and cause His crown to sparkle with jewels. You are to enrich his wealth with souls, fill his home with children, and the "many mansions" of heaven with the sorrowful ones of earth.[23]

## PREACHING: PREPARATION AND CONTENT

Just as some saints within our broader tradition have viewed askance those ministers who read prayers, scorn has been poured upon those who write out and read their sermons. In a letter of January 1859 to his sister, Marcia, Marcus Dods recounted his visit to a man who was drunk in bed. The man informed Dods that he had heard him preach—and then immediately corrected himself: "'Na, na,' (he was a Scotchman) 'ye didna preach, ye read.'"[24] J. M. Barrie's hapless probationer, Mr. Watts, lost a possible call to the Auld Licht Kirk because he read his sermon. In fact, "a breeze from heaven exposed him on the common."[25] The worthies had gathered on the common for an open-air service. In the travelling pulpit's two compartments sat Mr. Watts and Lang Tammas, "but no Auld Licht thought that it looked like a Punch and Judy puppet show."[26] There came a strong wind, and Mr. Watt's sermon, written on paper cut to the size of the pages of his Bible, were blown away, and his secret was out. Since "To follow a pastor who 'read' seemed to the Auld Lichts like claiming heaven on false pretences. . . . The minister was never seen in our parts again, but he is still remembered as 'Paper Watts.'"[27]

By contrast, the well-known and eccentric minister of Surrey Chapel, Rowland Hill, rounded upon a young preacher who wrote out his sermons:

23. Luke, *Memorials of F. W. Bourne*, 88–89.

24. Marcus Dods (son), ed., *Early Letters of Marcus Dods*, I, 122.

25. Barrie, *Auld Licht Idylls*, 74. The multiple Presbyterian secessions in eighteenth-century Scotland afford endless delight to church historians of a sturdy constitution.

26. Barrie, *Auld Licht Idylls*, 75.

27. Ibid., 77.

"It's a very bad custom, young gentleman; it's the worst thing you could do. Why don't you have more confidence in the Gospel?"[28] Hill at once proceeded to expound his own practice: "The Gospel is an excellent milk-cow. . . . I never write my sermons. I always trust to the Gospel. I first pull at justification, then give a plug at adoption, and afterwards tilt at sanctification, and so on until I have, in one way or another, filled my pail with Gospel milk."[29] Among the many ministers who feature in the folk memory of the Welsh is the one who explained, "There are three steps up to my pulpit, and every Sunday the Holy Spirit gives me a sermon point on every one." Further comment would be superfluous.

Preachers might well ponder Francis Bacon's advice: "Reading maketh a full man: Conference a ready man, and writing an exact man."[30] If sermons are written in full, the preacher should remember that the end product is not an essay with all the literary conventions that essay writing entails. John Flavel saw the point long ago: "He is the best artist, that can most lively and powerfully display Jesus Christ before the people, evidently setting forth as crucified among them; and that is the best sermon, that is most full of Christ, not of art and language."[31] On the other hand, if sermons are to be delivered from notes, or extempore, the preacher would do well to be cautioned by Augustine: one "who cannot speak both eloquently and wisely should speak wisely without eloquence, rather than eloquently without wisdom."[32] Whether sermons are written and read, or delivered extempore or from notes, diligent preparation is, in my view, essential. Bishop Ryle's reflection upon the carefully prepared sermons of Daniel Rowland makes the point: "The man who takes much pains with his sermons, and never brings out what has 'cost him nothing', is just the man I expect God will bless. We want well-beaten oil for the service of the sanctuary."[33]

It seems to me that one of the difficulties faced by preachers at the present time is that the amount of time the saints are able, or willing, to spend in worship and learning the faith has shrunk with the passage of time. When my ministry began, at least two services per Sunday were the norm in our churches, with the evening one sometimes being of a more

---

28. Grant, *The Metropolitan Pulpit*, 154.

29. Ibid., 155.

30. Bacon, *Essays*, no. 29, "Of Studies."

31. Flavel, *Works*, I, 39.

32. Augustine, *On Christian Doctrine*, II.iv.28.

33. Ryle, *Five Christian Leaders of the Eighteenth Century*, 102.

evangelistic nature. In many cases the Sunday services were supplemented by Bible study meetings which were not characterized by the casual, off-the-cuff chatting that some present-day house groups are prone to, but were genuine occasions for learning. Clearly, it is impossible for a preacher to achieve in one hour of worship all that could be accomplished in at least three hours. Is there a solution to this problem? Although it would require a culture change to obtain the outcome, I sometimes wonder whether some churches might consider a greater concentration of activity on Sunday mornings. I have in mind some transatlantic churches where the choir gathers for rehearsal at 8.30; there is an hour of Christian education for all ages from 9.30, with the service following at 11.00. Such a church in our context might, once per month/quarter conclude with a Jacob's Join/ Potluck lunch/Bring and Share meal at 12.30, followed by Church Meeting from 13.00 to 14.30. Such a programme would demonstrate the link between Church Meeting and public worship and also afford time for fellowship among the members. I also understand that when, as increasingly happens, pastorates comprise more than one church other arrangements would need to be made. The fact remains that adequate education of the flock (to which subject I shall return in the following chapter) cannot be achieved in the time allotted to the sermon; nor, indeed, is the sermon's primary purpose educational.

The most important thing is that in preaching the ministers get down to business and focus intently on the primary objective of preaching the gospel. A number of things can get in the way of this. Some ministers appear to have been taught that when preaching they must begin from where the people are. It is bordering on arrogance to assume that we know where every one of them is, and most ministers of this persuasion in fact descend into bland generalities—even in some cases into autobiography. I once heard a Christmas sermon in which it was only after we had spent more than half the sermon in the labour ward on the occasion of the minister's first child that we came within eyesight of the manger at Bethlehem. I do not wish to hear more about the minister's personal exploits than I hear about the gospel. It is an overstatement on his part, but sometimes it is difficult to suppress the memory of Daniel Jenkins's observation: "Few things have done more harm in modern England than the attitude of respectful docility with which Church people put up with incompetence and irrelevance from the pulpit."[34]

34. Jenkins, *The Protestant Ministry*, 192.

On the other hand, there are those who, by doing obeisance to the god Relevance, fall under the rod of Forsyth: "We must preach *to* our age, but woe to us if it is our age we preach, and only hold up a the mirror to the time."[35] Forsyth's student, Lovell Cocks, that kindest but most earnest of preachers, was similarly minded:

> [O]ur preaching has largely ceased to be theological and has become ethical in tone. . . . [P]eople are not being fed by our views on current events. It is necessary on occasion to preach peace and social reconstruction; it is necessary, on occasion, to castigate public evils like drink and gambling. But if we do nothing else we are not preaching the Word. We realise this and sometimes we sit down in our study and prepare to handle a great theme like Atonement or Justification by Faith. But the fire of inspiration will not burn; we cannot make the doctrine live even to ourselves, and the whole subject remains wooden and abstract. At last we find we have nothing to say and we fall back on a neat little address all about Martha and Mary, or a thoughtful essay on the psychology of habits. . . . And meanwhile the people come Sunday by Sunday—Oh! so patiently—waiting for the Word. God help us!—have we nothing to say?[36]

Again, there are ministers who think that they must lighten things up and amuse the saints. Samuel Bourn, the eighteenth-century Presbyterian divine, who never seemed happier than when teasing evangelical Baptists, wrote a dialogue in which the Baptist asks, "What think you now of our preachers?" The "Consistent Christian"—that is, Bourn, replies, "Tho' I approve of neither, yet I had rather see a *Statue* in the pulpit than a *Jack-pudding* or a *Merry Andrew*."[37] I well remember walking into a room where I was to have a meeting with two other ministers. They were equally able and loved, but they were poles apart in temperament: one was rumbustious, energetic and to the point; the other quiet, witty, and scholarly. The former was sounding off about one of the popular preachers of the day, and I had no difficulty in guessing which one it was. "A load of wind! His sermons are empty: just a string of cheerful little stories strung together by nothing in particular" came the stern judgment. When the critic paused for breath his colleague gently intervened: "But I'm told he executes a beautiful 'pause

35. Forsyth, *Positive Preaching and the Modern Mind*, 5.
36. Cocks, "By Faith Alone," typescript in Lovell Cocks papers.
37. Bourn, *A Dialogue between a Baptist and a Churchman*, 6.

for profile'!" As Forsyth drily remarked, "what is the use of captains who are more at home entertaining the passengers than navigating the ship?"[38]

With a view to varying the fare, some ministers are tempted to shun the sermon altogether in favour of dialogues, or religious drama or dance. I do not say that such things have no place in worship; intelligently handled they can supplement the preaching, but I do not think that they should replace the proclamation of the gospel by the one called to undertake this solemn yet exhilarating task. The main problem here is that ministers may think that the religious experience of the saints will necessarily be enhanced by such additions to the service, whereas I agree with P. T. Forsyth: "Look to the Gospel and it will see to the experiences."[39] Or perhaps they have fallen for the commercial line that the gospel is a product and we have to discover new ways of selling it. Forsyth had the answer to that too: "Our first business is neither to gather men nor to move them, but to preach in the speech of our time . . . the universal and moving Gospel. Let *it* gather them, and let *it* stir them."[40]

Finally, there are moral homilies which masquerade as sermons. In 1753, in what was not the only case of its kind, some of the church members at Sherborne, Dorset, who were dissatisfied "with the mild morality of [the Presbyterian] Mr. [William] Cornish's preaching" left to found a Congregational church.[41] In the following century Thomas de Quincey tells of the Rev. Samuel H., who belonged to the class of clerics

> who understand by religion simply a respectable code of ethics.
> . . . As a preacher, Mr. H., was sincere, but not earnest. . . . [I]t was
> impossible for any man, starting from the low ground of themes
> so unimpassioned and so desultory as the benefits of industry, the
> danger from bad companions, the importance of setting a good
> example, or the value of perseverance—to pump up any persistent
> stream of earnestness either in himself or in his auditors.[42]

In a letter of 22 April 1871 the future bishop, Mandell Creighton, offered his opinion of a sermon he heard Dean Stanley preach in the University Church of St. Mary, Oxford: "There was a certain amount of general moral enthusiasm, to the intent that it was desirable to be good rather than bad;

38. Forsyth, *Positive Preaching and the Modern Mind*, 101.
39. Forsyth, *Revelation Old and New*, 71.
40. Forsyth, *The Church, the Gospel and Society*, 115.
41. Densham and Ogle, *The Story of the Congregational Churches of Dorset*, 69.
42. de Quincey, *Confessions of an English Opium Eater*, (1856), 13.

but I had previously gathered that from other sources."[43] The Puritan Richard Sibbes was much wiser: "The preaching of mere morality, *if men be not careful to open Christ, to know how salvation is wrought by Christ, and how all good comes from Christ* . . . may make a man reform many abuses, like a philosopher, which hath its reward and respect amongst men, but nothing to give comfort at the hour of death and the day of judgment."[44] I have italicized the crucial words here; for sometimes the last thing sinners need is to be told what they ought to be doing. Sometimes this is the very thing they would love to do, but they are constrained. Paul was not alone in being able to testify that "The good which I want to do, I fail to do; but what I do is the wrong that is against my will" (Rom 7:19). What is required is not more moral exhortation, but rescue. For this very reason, as Paul discovered and as Sibbes knew well, God sent not one more teacher of morality, but a Saviour.

## EXPOSITION AND DOCTRINE

Exposition and doctrine are all too frequently the casualties where sermons of the types just discussed prevail. Indeed, I am sometimes tempted to think that expository sermons are increasingly rare in our churches, and if this is so it is very worrying. I state a fact, I do not extol my own homiletic efforts, but quite frequently as I go my itinerant way, people say, "Thank you for what you have said to us: it's such a long time since we heard a sermon like that." What have I been doing? Simply expounding a text or a passage with a view to proclaiming Christ and edifying the saints of whom I have been thinking during my preparation.[45] Whether a lectionary is used or not, there is ample scope for preachers to draw from the Bible a prophetic challenge, an evangelical summons, a word of consolation, a moral imperative, an encouragement to discipleship—the list of possible themes is vast—while at the same time treating these as implications of the gospel. Of Matthew Henry we learn that he "adhered with admirable closeness to the passage he professed to explain; neither, on the one hand, pressing into it

43. Creighton (wife), *Life and Letters of Mandell Creighton*, I. 92.

44. Sibbes, *Works*, I. 24, (my italics).

45. When visiting a church for the first time the situation is rather different. On one occasion, however, it transpired that I had, quite unwittingly, said something which, I was told, desperately needed to be said, and could hardly have been said by the regular minister who had to be there the following week!

service foreign or irrelevant truths, and still less far-fetched inventions; nor, on the other, evading any topick to which he was naturally led."[46] This is good advice, not least because it draws a clear distinction between exegesis, the drawing out from a text or passage what is there, and blatant eisegesis,[47] which is the reading into it of what is not there, of which the following is a cheerful example recounted by William Neil. A preacher took as his text, "Enoch walked with God; and he was not, for God took him" (which simply means that godly Enoch died).

> "Brethren," said the evangelist, "Holy Scripture tells us that Enoch was not. What was he not? I will tell you. He was not an Episcopalian, for he walked and didn't dance. He was not a Baptist, for he walked and didn't swim. He was not a Presbyterian because he walked with God. Hallelujah, brethren, he was a Methodist, for the Lord took him."[48]

As for doctrine, in the eighteenth century this was frequently the cause, or sometimes, perhaps, the pretext, of secessions from Dissenting churches. In some cases those of a more evangelical turn of mind did not hear the "language of Canaan" to which they had been accustomed from ministers who were tending in a heterodox direction, while on the other hand, some churches became oppressed by ministers who had, in their view, become tainted by the enthusiasm of the Methodist revival. Presbyterians tended more frequently in the former direction, Congregationalists in the latter, but in either case secessions occurred, and there was a re-shaping of church life on the ground such that by the end of the century most Presbyterian churches had become Congregationalist, while a significant number of them had become Unitarian. Some preachers did not think that the pulpit was the place for parading their doctrinal party views, whether they were Calvinistic, Arminian, or Unitarian, while others had no scruples on the matter. The latter kind could all too easily be at the mercy of saints whose doctrinal antennae were finely tuned—like those of J. M. Barrie's Auld Lichts. "For the first year or more of his ministry," we learn, "an Auld Licht minister was a mouse among cats.

---

46. J. B. Williams, *Memoirs of the Life, Character, and Writings of the Rev. Matthew Henry*, (1828), Edinburgh: The Banner of Truth Trust, 1972, 122.

47. I say "*blatant* eisegesis" because no exegesis is entirely innocent of interpretation, for we all bring our presuppositions to the text. But "blatant eisegesis" is the art of finding in a text what no reasonable person of integrity could possibly find in it.

48. Neil, *The Plain Man Looks at the Bible*, 113.

Both in the pulpit and out of it they watched for unsound doctrine, and when he strayed they took him by the neck."[49]

As with questions of biblical criticism, so with doctrine. A sermon is not the place for a harangues on doctrinal party points—spurious victories indeed if the opposing party is not present, or is sufficiently well behaved as to be silent. In his ordination charge of 1722 to Micaijah Towgood the Presbyterian John Withers declared,

> I conceive the weighty Matters of the Gospel, Repentance towards God, and Faith in the Lord Jesus Christ, ought principally to be insisted on. Your Business is not to fill Mens heads with nice and useless Speculations. . . . Not to make Men subtil Disputants, but exact and holy Walkers. . . . We should insist on the great and weighty *Matters of the Law, Faith, Judgment* and *Mercy*; not the *Annise, Mint* and *Cummin*, that grew in our own Gardens.[50]

Clearly, to take such advice is not to dispense with doctrine altogether. On the contrary, in the opinion of Erasmus, "The Minister is then in the very height of his dignity, when from the pulpit he feeds the Lord's flock with sacred doctrine."[51] I cannot help wondering where, for example, have gone the sermons on adoption, regeneration, justification by grace through faith, sanctification, and even on the cross? I hear much about the hungry, abused and bullied; I am exhorted to be a peacemaker, to crusade for justice, and to be hospitable to all. But if this is not to be bland humanism, where is the convictional basis, and whence comes the necessary power?

I have heard ministers say that people no longer have the language of doctrine on the tip of their tongues. Their response is to leave doctrine alone. Mine is to teach the people, for I agree with Daniel Jenkins that "One of the first fruits of a true revival of faith must always be a revival of the vigour of Christian language."[52] If, as was said, the barbers in Alexandria of old were discussing the Trinity; if humble lay preachers of my youth could accurately employ doctrinal terms, I see no reason why ministers should refrain from explaining and using them. The saints are not fools, and they do not need to be patronized. Many of them have mastered computer terms, and some of them can even comprehend marketing-speak! The saints, no

49. Barrie, *Auld Licht Idylls*, 79.

50. Withers, *A Charge Given to Mr. Micaijah Towgood*, 19–20.

51. Erasmus, *Ecclesiastes*, I.

52. Jenkins, *The Gift of Ministry*, 148. See further, Sell, *Nonconformist Theology in the Twentieth Century*, 165–70.

less than the minister, have a responsibility in this matter, and Baxter pulled no punches: "Were you but as willing to get the knowledge of God and heavenly things as you are to know how to work in your trade, you would have set yourself to it before this day, and you would have spared no cost or pains till you had got it. But you account seven years little enough to learn your trade, and will not bestow one day in seven in diligent learning the matters of your salvation."[53]

It would seem that some people will do all they can to avoid doctrine. I have even heard the slogan, "Not doctrine, but spirituality." This is reminiscent of such hoary slogans as "Not doctrine, but service" and "Not creed, but life." Principal D. W. Simon of Spring Hill College, Birmingham girded his loins against such effete effusions in his address on the occasion of the opening of the new and enlarged buildings of Lancashire Independent College in 1878, of which he was an alumnus. What he says is the more telling because he was speaking in what we, with hindsight, regard as the heyday of Nonconformity:

> The Congregationalists of the present day are in no small danger of disintegrating—both as individual Churches and as an association of Churches. . . . We are told . . . that the true, if indeed not the only basis, of Christian union is sentiment, feeling, emotion, and life. Doctrine and system are scouted as things which divide those who at heart are agreed. My reading of the history of the Church, both at home and abroad, leads me to a different conclusion. No communities fall to pieces so quickly as those which have no tie but sentiment, whereas communities which are welded together by convictions as well as by feelings, resist attack alike from within and from without.[54]

As a protest against any suggestion that people are saved by subscription to statements of doctrine, some of them with numerous sub-clauses— which position can issue in a hard, exclusive, self-righteous sectarianism, which is not at all what Simon was intending to commend—the sloganizing was understandable. The attitude expressed is not, however, justifiable. For, by grace, the saints know whom they have believed, and doctrine is the articulation of belief, and without it witness is impossible. If someone testifies, "Jesus is my Lord and Saviour," we already have a summary announcement of three central doctrines: those concerning the person and work of

---

53. Baxter, *Practical Works*, VII, 269.
54. Simon, "Theological Training for Ministerial Students," 91.

Christ and needy humanity. The truth is that doctrine, at the heart of which is the good news of Jesus Christ, feeds spirituality, impels us into service, and requires a life consistent with our profession of faith.

I am the first to agree that we cannot express our doctrines in exactly the way our forebears did. For one thing, since we live on our side of modern biblical criticism we cannot pile up proof texts as they did; for another, our attention is drawn by our context to things which they cannot be blamed for not having foreseen. Some of the Reformed doctrinal treatises are highly complex, and some of their conclusions are highly debatable. Forsyth had such contributions in mind when he said, "Reduce the burden of belief we must. The old orthodoxy laid on men's believing power more than it could carry."[55] But he also had no patience with humanizing liberals: "Too many are occupied in throwing over precious cargo; they are lightening the ship even of its fuel."[56]

The upshot is that the preacher is not in the pulpit in order to deliver a doctrinal lecture, but if the Bible is fairly expounded, doctrine will be unavoidable, for the Scriptures are full of it. More than that, however: the doctrine is the product of the experience of early Christians of the saving grace and constant presence of Christ. Far from being products of a dry intellectual pursuit, the doctrinal affirmations were personal testimonies to the mighty works of God in creation and redemption. If our preachers, and if the saints, are truly united with Christ they will find themselves speaking doctrine, perhaps even despite themselves.

## A MISCELLANY OF CAUTIONS

Although this is not a manual of homiletics, I do not think it inappropriate to offer a few reminders from the past regarding the delivery of sermons. Of Philip Henry it was said that

> He adapted his method and style to the capacities of his hearers, fetching his similitudes for illustration from those things which were familiar to them. He did not shoot the arrow of the word over their heads in high notions, or the flourishes of affected rhetorick, nor under their feet, by blunt and homely expressions, as many do under the pretence of plainness, but to their hearts in close and lively applications. His delivery was very graceful and agreeable,

55. Forsyth, *Positive Preaching and the Modern Mind*, 84.
56. Forsyth, *The Principle of Authority*, 261.

far from being either noisy and precipitate on the one hand, or dull and slow on the other.[57]

Not all preachers have been as wise as Henry. In the nineteenth century Henry Rogers teased users of high-flown language with good reason. He had little patience with those for whom

'Heat' straightway becomes 'calorific,' lightening the 'electric fluid'; instead of plants and animals, we are surrounded by 'organised substances'; life is nothing half so good as the 'vital principle'; 'phenomena' of all kinds are very plentiful; these phenomena are 'developed' and 'combined' and 'analysed,' and, in short, done everything with, except being made intelligible.[58]

On one occasion George Reindorp prevented an homiletic atrocity. He managed to prevent a curate from bringing an erudite passage to a triumphant conclusion, thus: "and so it will be seen that, contrary to expectation, these two opposing hypotheses can, unexpectedly, co-habit."[59]

Preachers who delight in blinding their hearers with science are not yet extinct from the earth. I well recall a sermon by a distinguished professor of theology, which included untranslated quotations from Latin, Greek and German. There was no need for this: it was a dereliction of duty and, generously supposing that the lexical incomprehensibility was not motivated by downright arrogance, the excuse of professorial eccentricity, had it been advanced, would not have been acceptable. Not without good reason did John Eachard trounce preachers who employ an "abundance of Greek and Latin," and "swagger also over their poor parishioners with the dreadful Hebrew itself."[60] It is reported that the elderly scholar Martin Routh said to a congregation of humble hearers, "I know, my friends, you will object to me what St. Irenaeus says"—and proceeded to quote the second-century theologian to them.[61] It is not impossible that Bernard Lord Manning's curt recommendation was stimulated by distressing experience: "Banish every expression coined by psychologists."[62] Of Paul Cardale, Presbyterian

57. M. Henry, *The Life of the Rev. Philip Henry, A.M.*, 59–60.

58. Rogers, *Essays*, I, 416.

59. Reindorp, *Putting it Over*, recalled from memory.

60. Eachard, *The Grounds and Occasions of the Contempt of the Clergy and Religion Enquired Into*, I, 37.

61. See McLachlan, *Essays and Addresses*, 274, 345.

62. Manning, *A Layman in the Ministry*, 146.

minister at Evesham, Job Orton observed that he "ruined a fine congregation by his very learned, dry and critical discourses, an extreme heaviness in the pulpit, and an almost total neglect of pastoral visits and private inspection."[63]

Accounts of the undue length of sermons are legion. One of John Howe's female hearers lamented that, "Mr. Howe is so long laying out the cloth that I despair of the dinner."[64] Who cannot feel for a son of Richard Tyrer, a nineteenth-century minister of Darlington Street Wesleyan Church, Wolverhampton? His muse prompted him thus:

> Plague on the parson's lengthy tongue;
> He spins his sermons out too long;
> The pudding's spoilt, the meat's o'erdone,
> The 'taters have to water run.[65]

Of his afternoon congregation at Stand Unitarian Church, Philip Pearsall Carpenter declared, with reference to his extempore sermons, "The people certainly prick up their ears when they see me put my watch on the pulpit, and not light the candles."[66]

Today we are sometimes told that people cannot listen for long: they are so accustomed to sound-bites. Let us take care that we do not patronize the saints. They may well be tired of sermons; I seriously question whether they are tired of the gospel. On the contrary, they can be held by it, and even yearn for more of it; and that not because of oratorical excellence or pulpit histrionics, but because God the Holy Spirit is addressing them, challenging them, consoling them, through it. The most telling sermons I ever heard were those of a minister whose grasp of the gospel was secure, whose love for the saints was evident, whose sincerity shone through all he did, and who expounded texts carefully and illustrated his points aptly, all the while speaking quietly, humbly and thoughtfully, but to great effect. We never thought that his sermons were too long.

Few packed so much homiletic advice into one long paragraph as the Presbyterian divine, Samuel Chandler. He sums up much of what I have tried to say, and I extract the following points:

---

63. Orton, *Letters to Dissenting Ministers*, I, 154.
64. Quoted by Poole-Connor, *Evangelicalism in England*, 125.
65. Pratt, *Black Country Methodism*, 57.
66. McLachlan, *Essays and Addresses*, 126.

Christ the wisdom and power of God, should be the motto of a Christian pastor, the sentiment of his heart, and the governing subject of his preaching. But if we preach ourselves, our own speculations, our philosophical subtleties, or our secular interests; if leaving the plain practical doctrines of Christ, we preach unintelligible, abstruse, mysterious points; . . . if we press any party-explication of them, as necessary to communion and salvation, and thereby create disturbances and schisms in the church; . . . if we enter into political debates, and the low spirit of faction; if we preach up our own divine prerogatives and powers, our authority over the flock, our being lords of the heritage; . . . or if in preaching the truth, we make use of unintelligible terms, quaint phrases, swelling words, false rhetorick, odd gestures, ridiculous actions, violent agitations, distortions of the face, and the like unnatural peculiarities; or if we condescend to love expressions . . . ; if we abuse and pervert scripture, fetch doctrines from texts that God never put into them, and endeavour to prove points by strained and torturous applications of scripture . . these and like methods will expose us to contempt, and justly fix on us the charge of the foolishness of preaching.[67]

## PASTORAL CARE

It should be clear by now that there can be no hard and fast distinction between preaching from pastoral care. For preaching is pastoral work; and the pastoral care of the flock is with a view to the upbuilding of the saints in the faith as they face the particular issues of life that confront them. The unfaithful shepherds of Jeremiah's day did not only fail to feed the flock; they destroyed it, allowed it to scatter, and had no care for its members. Ezekiel, no less than Jeremiah, believed that God would visit his people and rescue his flock: "As a shepherd goes in search of his sheep when his flock is scattered from him in every direction, so I shall go in search of my sheep and rescue them. . . . I shall search for the lost, recover the straggler, bandage the injured, strengthen the sick, leave the healthy and strong to play, and give my flock their proper food" (Ezek 34:11, 16). This seems to me to be a fairly comprehensive statement of the pastor's role, and it would appear that Oliver Goldsmith's village preacher rose to the challenge, for

in his duty, prompt at every call,

67. Chandler, *Preaching the Gospel a More Effectual Method of Salvation, than Human Wisdom*, 57–58

He watched and wept, and prayed and felt, for all.[68]

As with the feeding of the flock, the caring of it is the privilege of the under-shepherds of the Good Shepherd, the Head of the church. The feeding and the caring together are of central importance in Christian ministry. John Owen concurs: "The first and principal duty of a pastor is to *feed the flock* by the diligent preaching of the word. . . . This work and duty . . . is essential unto the office of a pastor. A man is a pastor unto them whom he feeds by pastoral teaching . . . and he that doth not so feed is no pastor."[69] Ministers may do many other things, but if they are not holding these two obligations of preaching and pastoral care together, or if they major on one at the expense of the other, serious questions of vocation are raised.

From time to time ministers tell me that nowadays they do not have time for pastoral visitation because they have so many meetings to attend. I have even been told that ministers are much busier now than in the past. This is, frankly, silly. If a minister of today is working a twelve-hour day he or she is no busier than one who was doing the same thing fifty years ago. The questions are, what is being done in the available time? Do all of the meetings concern matters central to their role? Should some of them be attended by other church members? The saddest aspect of the plea that there is no time for pastoral visitation is that if it really is the case, opportunities of sharing the gospel in the places where the saints spend their days are lost. I hesitate to use the word "catechetics" because many seem, wrongly, to understand it to mean indoctrination. Be that as it may, Thomas Watson fully understood that if this task were neglected, Christians would be "unsettled in religion. . . . As feathers will be blown every way, so with feathery Christians."[70] The very busy and prolific Richard Baxter put much time and effort into catechising the church members and their children: "Two days every week my assistant and I myself took fourteen families between us for private catechising and conference (he going through the parish, and the town coming to me)."[71] Two centuries on we find J. A. Macfadyen, the first minister of Chorlton Road Congregational Church, Manchester, undertaking his teaching duties according to a plan devised with *quasi*-military precision. He paid particular attention to the children and young people because of "my deep conviction of the important relationship entered into between

68. Goldsmith, "The Deserted Village," lines 165–66.

69. Owen, *Works*, XVI, 74, 75.

70. Watson, *A Body of Divinity*, 1.

71. Baxter, *Autobiography*, 77–78.

the Church and the child in baptism."[72] He believed that the teaching of
the faith in the home was of primary importance, followed by that in the
Sunday school. To this the pastor's teaching was supplementary, and it was
not intended to replace pastoral visitation, for children and young people
would welcome into their homes ministers whom they had come to know
in the classroom. In addition to classes for the various age groups, the catechumens' class was attended by sixty to eighty young people. Here "[t]he
subjects treated were personal religion, and so much of Congregational
polity as might prepare them to be intelligent members of the Church."[73]

Whatever word we use to describe the minister's pastoral-cum-
teaching role, and wherever the task is performed, at the heart of it is the
confirmation of the saints, and the nurture of the young, in the faith, and
the personal communication of the gospel to them with specific relation to
their lives and circumstances. As the hymn says,

> some are sick, and some are sad,
> and some have never loved you well,
> and some have lost the love they had;
> and some are pressed with worldly care,
> and some are tried with fear and doubt,
> and some such grievous passions tear,
> that only you can cast them out;
> and none, O Lord, have perfect rest,
> for none are wholly free from sin;
> and those who long to serve you best
> are conscious most of wrong within.[74]

If Henry Twells were living now he might have added that some are un-
employed, some are hungry in a land of plenty, some are greedy, some are
betrayed, some are refugees, and some are lonely. If pastoral realism had
really overcome him, he might even have noted (or tactfully have avoided
noting) that some are downright cussed. But there they all are, and all to
be loved for Christ's sake, each one needing to be encouraged in Christian
witness and service, each one needing to gain in Christian confidence, each

---

72. Mackennal, *Life of John Allison Macfadyen*, 128; cf. 168.

73. Ibid., 131.

74. "At evening, when the sun was set," *Rejoice and Sing*, no. 644.

one needing to be helped to exercise their gifts and fulfil the particular ministry to which they have been called.

Nor should questions of the discipline required to build up the flock be overlooked. The pastoral visits of John Boyce to his flock of Presbyterian pioneers of Pisgah in the Arkansas River Valley were fondly remembered fifty years after they were made: "His visits were very satisfactory to the church especially as he was very pointed in reminding the heads of families of their duties and conversed with the young concerning their spiritual interests."[75] B. C. Plowright spoke wisely when, more than fifty years ago, he observed that "It may and does run counter to much conventional thought about the ministry at the present time, but we are, in fact, nowhere so truly incarnational in our ministry as when we meet our people in their own homes and in the setting of their ordinary surroundings."[76] Apart from any loss to the saints, if ministers neglect the pastoral task they themselves miss so much, and their preaching is less well informed than it otherwise would be. Again, ministers are called to model the pastoral office before the members in general and the elders in particular; for elders need to be encouraged and supported in their pastoral role, which they are called to exercise as companions of ministers, not as their substitutes.

I think it well that ministers who are too busy to offer pastoral care to the flock reflect seriously upon their situation. We shall all be asked to give an account of those who were committed to our charge (Heb 13:17). This prospect is awesome, as William Bagshawe fully understood: "When ministers think of the preciousness of one soul, and their being charged with many, may not every one of them cry out with St. Paul: 'Who is sufficient for these things?'" At the same time, he testifies that "there is a sufficiency (yea, all-sufficiency) in divine grace."[77] If further motivation be required, Richard Baxter will supply it. Thinking of those in a minister's care, he imagines Christ asking, "Did I die for them, and wilt thou not look after them? Were they worth my blood, and are they not worth thy labour? Did I come down from heaven to earth, to seek and save that which was lost; and wilt thou not go to the next door, or street, or village to seek them? . . . I debased myself to this, but it is thy honour to be so employed."[78] Of William

75. Ragsdale, *They Sought a Land: A Settlement in the Arkansas River Valley 1840–1870*, 40.

76. Plowright, "The Holy Spirit in the Work of the Ministry," 151.

77. Brentall, *William Bagshawe*, 112.

78. Baxter, *Gildas Salvianus. The Reformed Pastor*, 297.

Grimshaw it is written that he would "walk several miles in the night, in storms of snow, when few people would venture out of their doors, to visit a sick person."[79] Would we, with our cars, do as much—even in summer-time?

The solemn words of Matthew 25:31–46 must surely come home with particular force to those of us who serve as Christ's pastoral under-shepherds. It goes without saying that apart from the head Shepherd's constant companionship we could not even make a start. In one of his hymns George Burder, the itinerant preacher, settled pastor, secretary of the London Missionary Society, editor of the *Evangelical* Magazine—and much else besides, saw the point:

> The work begun is carried on
> By power from heaven above;
> And every step, from first to last,
> Proclaims that God is love!

By God's gracious call ministers of the gospel stand in the apostolic succession of those who both feed and care for Christ's flock. And when we fail, as we shall, or deny him, as Peter the rock-man did, what does he do? He simply comes to us again and says, "Feed my lambs, tend my sheep" (John 21:15–16). More than that: the good Shepherd, who calls us by name, and whose voice we recognize, "ever lives to make intercession for us" (Heb 7:25). Sustained by his prayers we can go about our pastoral duties confident that "when the chief shepherd appears [we, by God's grace and mercy,] will receive glory, a crown that never fades" (1 Pet 5:4).

79. Newton, *Memoirs of the Life of the Late William Grimshaw*, 102.

# 5

# The Education of the Ministers

In this chapter I have in mind not only the ministers of the gospel, but the ministries of all the visible saints. What do the church members need to know? What education do the ministers of the gospel need if they are to undertake not only their educational task (which is of vital importance, and will not necessarily be accomplished by farming people out into house groups), but also the liturgical, preaching, and pastoral duties that we have already discussed?

## THE CHRISTIAN EDUCATION OF THE SAINTS

I think of a large down-town church in an English industrial town. The building has seen better days, and in a dark and rather forbidding room in its nether regions there hangs a poster, slightly tattered and yellowed with age. It dates from about 1930, and it bears the message, "The children of today are the church of tomorrow." It is not the best theology, for the baptized children of today are *already* within the covenant family of the church. My main point, though, is that if the poster were designed to be prophetic, then the prophecy has not been fulfilled in most of our churches. Sad to say, the twenty people who worship in that large tabernacle give the lie to their own publicity. In 1930 the Congregational Union of England and Wales, to which they then belonged, counted 331,719 church members and about 433,786 children in its Sunday Schools. By some sort of geometrical progression there should by now be hundreds of thousands of church members in that denomination. In fact, in 2012, after three church unions The United Reformed Church had 61,627 church members and 15,504 "Children in Worship."

It is not difficult to specify a number of causes for the statistical decline, but one of them may very well be the neglect of adult education in our churches, and the resultant tongue-tied-ness of parents as regards the Christian nurture of their children. This is connected with a crisis of faith of significant proportions. We shall never know how many people quietly drifted from our churches because they were never helped towards a mature faith. Perhaps they found nobody to help them; perhaps they thought that if they expressed their doubts they would be viewed askance by the pious ones. In either case, they thought that they were expected to believe what they could not believe; and the sad thing is that much of what they thought they had to believe some, perhaps most, ministers did not believe either, but they never said so. There is evidence to suggest that in many cases the last time some church members received consistent Christian education was during their confirmation/membership classes. We have much ground to make up, and I offer the following suggestions which have been prompted by what church members have said to me in various places.

First, church members need help to read and understand the Bible. Some are, of course, knowledgeable Bible students, others regularly read the Bible, perhaps following one of the courses of study that are widely available. But many are all at sea. As far as the Old Testament is concerned some can perhaps remember the bits they used to draw in Sunday School—Noah in the ark, Moses in the bulrushes, Daniel in the lion's den; and from the New Testament they may recall some of the stories of Jesus, whilst being completely stumped by Revelation. They need help to navigate what is a remarkable collection of texts written and compiled over a period of a thousand years by many hands. The worldview is that of the ancient Near East; the material is not presented chronologically, and in character it is varied in style and type: we have narrative, history, laws, doctrine, poetry, prophecy, and parables. How are people to find their way about such a collection? I have found that church members can become quite excited by some of the detective work which is thrown up by Bible study. The nature of the early chapters of Genesis; the make-up and dating of the Pentateuch; the purpose of Ruth and Jonah; the contrasting messages of the prophets; the poetry of the Psalms; the synoptic problem; the infancy narratives; Paul and James on grace and works; Revelation as underground literature—all of these topics, and many more, can come as stimulating and refreshing news to many of our people.

Then there are the questions that may be asked of individual passages. What kind of literature is this? What do we think the writer wished to convey to his own generation? Does what is written have a word for us today? If our honest answer to the third question is that we cannot divine any meaning for us from a particular portion of Scripture, let us not be downcast. We are not bound by the ritual laws of the Old Testament; large tracts of genealogy may appear to have no immediate relevance to us; not all of the moral judgments of biblical characters are to be endorsed by us. But the unworthy views of God, the violent acts and immorality are all part and parcel of the context within which God was nurturing his people; and they were falteringly finding their way, just as we do, for none of these things have vanished from the face of the earth.

The history of the transmission of the Bible is a further exciting tale to be told. But what is of supreme importance is that church members are encouraged to see that while the books of the Bible need to be read against the background of their times, they also need to be read in the light of what God has supremely said and done in Jesus Christ. He is God's final word to us—not in the sense of God's last word to us, but in the sense of his supreme word. By this I mean that we shall never know more about God than we see in Jesus Christ. In him God has wrought the victory over sin and death. Thus, on the one hand, there is no need to reduce the Bible to a list of purple passages (*The Bible Designed to be Read as Literature*—which it never was): in fact this would be to misunderstand its purpose. For one thing, by editing out all the sinners there would be no room for us! Nor, on the other hand, do we need to supplement the Bible, for once the infant church is on its missionary way, all the rest is commentary. We simply need to discern the word of God in the Bible we have, and to view it all in the light of God's self-revelation in Jesus Christ. Our ministers are there to guide us in this exciting voyage of discovery.

Secondly, the saints need to be thoroughly taught, and to have the opportunity of discussing, the doctrines of the Christian faith. Ideally, this will involve drawing critically on the heritage of Christian thought—not excluding classical and more recent Reformed confessions of faith. Such a course will almost certainly throw up such challenges to Christian belief as are exemplified by the age-old questions, "Why do the righteous suffer?" "How can we believe in a God of love when $x$, $y$, $z$ happen?" When such challenges come from those to whom we seek to witness, we are in the realm of apologetics. When they are posed by our Christian friends their pastoral implications are clear. At once we see that a course on Christian doctrine is more than a matter of imparting of information. It enables us to offer a more confident account of what we believe than we otherwise might, and in times of personal tragedy it strengthens our grasp upon the convictions that will help us through. More than that: I firmly believe that the study of Christian doctrine in the way I have suggested, can strengthen the devotional life of the saints.[1]

Thirdly, church members have told me that they need help and encouragement in their devotional life. The help they need is of at least two kinds. First, they need to see the purpose of prayer, and this sometimes means having misunderstandings removed. If we think of prayer as appropriate only in desperate times, we have not really grasped its meaning. "To prayers, to prayers! All lost! To prayers, to prayers! All lost!" cried Shakespeare's shipwrecked sailors in *The Tempest*.[2] I am sure that God hears sincere SOS prayers; and I recall the claim that "The creed of the English is that there is no God, and that it is advisable to pray to him from time to time." My point is that, as we saw in chapter 3, the range of prayer is much wider than this. Prayer is communion with God—verbally or in silence; and when we think of God's nature, holiness, and grace, do not all the parts of prayer come to mind: adoration, confession, supplication, thanksgiving, intercession, and consecration? Secondly—and this is where the pastoral shoe pinches—ministers need to be able to offer more than bland platitudes when people say, "I prayed sincerely, but God did nothing!" Thirdly, when we have grasped the purpose and types of prayer, the challenge is not over. How are our people to practice a life of prayer? Breakfast in shifts; overloaded diaries; family members who may not profess the Christian, or any other, faith—how far can our homes be places of prayer?

Fourthly, I think it important that church members understand something of the Reformed family into which they have come. In our family we believe, among other things, that God is sovereign in creation and redemption; that salvation is by grace through faith; that good works flow from, but are not the cause of, the new life in Christ which is union with him and with

---

1. So strongly do I believe this that I tried my hand at a trilogy, written for ministers, church members, and enquirers, entitled, *Doctrine and Devotion*. The three volumes are, *God Our Father*, *Christ Our Saviour*, *The Spirit Our Life*.

2. Shakespeare, *The Tempest*, I.i.

all his people grounded upon his saving act at the Cross; that God the Holy Spirit calls out and gathers one church, enabling our response of faith; and that by the same Spirit the church is ever in need of being reformed. Rooted in the Bible, regarding our confessions of faith as signposts, we seek the Spirit's guidance to do in our time what our forebears did in theirs, namely, to confess Christ and to make a credible witness to God's saving grace.[3]

It goes without saying that the interpretation of these truths has varied through time in relation to the specific contexts in which Christians have found themselves. As I noted earlier, we stand on our side of modern biblical criticism, and we cannot use the Bible as a collection of proof texts in the way that some of our forebears did. Again, those in this country to whom we in The United Reformed Church are heirs, were prompted by political circumstances to emphasize the fact that freedom is freedom by in and for the gospel (it is not freedom from it), and that "the Lord Jesus Christ, the only king and head of the Church, has therein appointed a government distinct from civil government and in things spiritual not subordinate thereto . . ."[4]

I know very well that many people in a consumerist age seek out a church for reasons other than its doctrinal stance or convictional heritage. But we of The United Reformed Church are people who stand for certain doctrines and principles that we hold dear, and if people seek membership with us, we owe it to them to explain our beliefs and our ways—otherwise we cheat them and do not give them the basis of belief and churchmanship for their ministry in, and their mission beyond, our churches.

The question sometimes arises, Is it really polite, in these ecumenical times, to harp on about our doctrinal distinctives? I believe that it is essential, and I speak as one whose United Reformed church membership is held in formal and annually-renewed covenant with Roman Catholics, members of the Church of England, Baptists, and Methodists. We are a melting-pot of Christian traditions, but at the same time we recognize our unity in Christ, and we worship and witness together. I believe that those wishing to be received as members or to confirm their faith in our midst ought to be instructed not only in basic Christian doctrines, but also in the heritage of the five covenanted traditions, for people need to know that into which they are being engrafted, so that as they grow in our midst they will

3. See further, Sell, *Confessing the Faith Yesterday and Today*, ch. 1.
4. Bush, *The United Reformed Church . . . The Manual*, 20.

come to appreciate more fully both what holds us all together, and what each tradition contributes to the whole.

As a footnote to this point I would add that in my judgment ministers who are called or appointed to serve in ecumenical partnerships should likewise attend a short course of induction into the history and ways of the partner churches. Furthermore, ministers coming to serve The United Reformed Church from other nations, not least from other Reformed churches, ought to be similarly helped. The ethos of one church, even within the Reformed family, can differ significantly from that of another; and some Reformed ministers are as likely to be puzzled as to the nature and purpose of Church Meeting, for example, as clergy of the Church of England and priests of the Roman Catholic Church. It goes without saying that ministers of The United Reformed Church should similarly be required to become acquainted with the history and ways of those traditions with whom they will be working in ecumenical partnership.

Fifthly, church members need opportunities of discussing the thicket of issues which travel under the umbrella of personal and social ethics. Let us think of so-called personal ethical issues. I say "so-called" because I wonder whether any ethical issues are ever exclusively personal; certainly they are not private. I have conducted degree courses in ethics, and I have noticed that even Christian students—not least Christian students who attend Bible study meetings—can sound just like humanists when they consider the propriety or otherwise of certain courses of action. In chorus, Christians and humanists alike will say, "Well, so long as you're not hurting anyone else . . ." Where is the transcendent reference? Where is the notion of living under the aspect of eternity?

To take one example of a so-called personal ethical issue: non-medically prescribed drugs, amongst which I include alcohol and nicotine. Sometimes the first hurdle is to persuade people that decision is called for in this matter: whether under peer pressure or not, they slide into a pattern of activity as if they had no choice. Having gained agreement that this is a subject for rational argument and choice, the next thing is to resist any desire to proceed by hurling biblical texts around. This is not the way to treat the Bible, and if it were we should frequently be at a loss: the Bible will not tell me whether I ought to donate a kidney to a known alcoholic, for it knows nothing of kidney donation. No, the first requirement is for facts about non-medically-prescribed drugs. What do they do to people? What are the likely or possible consequences of taking them? Who are we supporting by purchasing them? We might then proceed to reflect upon the distinction between what is morally right and what is legally permissible. From the fact that the law permits the sale and use of some non-medically prescribed drugs it does not follow that it is right to use them, still less that we are obliged to use them.

We might then turn to the Bible and look not for explicit commands, but for applicable principles. We shall soon find that nowhere in the Bible is there the suggestion that salvation depends upon the renunciation of drugs. Salvation is unconditional and free. But having begun a new life in Christ we may well wish, and need, to review past practice; but this will be a product of our new vitality, not a bargaining counter for gaining it. Furthermore, we may not give others the impression that Christianity is a new legalism, or that admission to church membership requires the endorsement of a specific set of ethical choices—that way lies sectarianism. What I think we shall find if we diligently search the Scriptures is a set of guiding principles which we may apply to the question of drugs. We will find out whose we are; we will learn that our bodies are to be temples of the Holy Spirit; we will recall that we are to love our neighbour as we have been loved; we will be reminded of our obligation to weaker brothers and sisters, and also of the peril of those who put stumbling-blocks in the path of others; and we will learn something of our vocation as stewards of God's creation. In the light of such considerations we shall make our decision and, if we are wise, we shall at the same time pray to be saved from an uncharitable, holier-than-thou, disposition towards those who differ from us.

I called the question of non-medically prescribed drugs a personal issue, whilst also querying that description, and for good reason. For when we think of the cost and the strain on health services which results from the abuse of drugs; the days lost from work; the road accidents caused; the strain imposed upon family members and others; we begin to see that the social implications are serious and far-reaching. But I suppose that matters which are traditionally regarded as belonging to social ethics would include problems arising within the economic order, politics, peace and war, and the like. Here too are subjects on which Christian reflection is needed. I do not say that every Christian can, or needs to, master the technicalities with underlie some highly complex matters. But sometimes our Church refers to the membership documents relating to justice, poverty, human trafficking, and usually the issues are clearly stated. Why should church members not have the opportunity of reflecting together on such matters? Indeed, taking action by prayer, gifts, approaching members of parliament, could well be part of the mission of the local church, as well as of the wider councils of the church. If salvation has to do with the whole person, and with the whole of life, we cannot be indifferent to the needs of others, to the threats under which millions live, and to the economic exploitation, whether from afar of near to home, that forces the deprivation of basic necessities upon those who are, in worldly terms, powerless. Informed Christian opinion is the springboard to the church's prophetic mission in society.

Finally, people in our churches need help in facing the issues of life, and of these, paradoxically, the most important, and the most frequently neglected, is that of death. It is as if we know, intellectually, that there is nothing surer than that we shall die, but we do not wish to dwell upon the matter. We raid the Latin so that we can speak of morticians rather than of death-handlers; and have you noticed how often, when the word "death" comes along the line of a hymn, the organist damps everything down into a godly hush—even in the metrical version of Psalm 23, where vanquished death should be sung about in tones of godly defiance:

> Yea, though I walk through death's dark vale
> Yet will I fear no ill
> For thou art with me . . .

Of course death is solemn. Of course the physical parting from loved ones is painful. Of course those who mourn must be allowed to express their grief, and must be ministered to with the most loving pastoral care of which we are capable—which requires the shunning of such banal and actually hurtful platitudes as, "God loved him/her more than you did, so took him/her home." Nevertheless we do have hope. Christ is victorious. The last enemy is vanquished. There is nothing which can separate us from God's love in Christ (Rom 8:31–39). These themes need to be brought home to young and old alike, for whether we are young or old, we do not have all the time in the world; we have just the time we are given. It matters how we live; it matters how we die. The Calvinist, A. M. Toplady, used to speak of "the euthanasia [dying well] of Christians," and John Wesley the evangelical Arminian likewise said of the Methodists, "Our people die well." I like the attitude of that eccentric preacher, Rowland Hill. When he was over eighty years of age he met an acquaintance who was nearly as old as himself, and said, "'If you and I don't march off soon, our friends yonder,' (looking upwards) 'will think we have lost our way.'"[5]

5. Jay, *Autobiography*, 359.

"Our friends yonder." That is the point. We do not go into strange territory. We go with Christ to be with friends. Richard Baxter made a long list of sixty-two saints of all ages whom he was looking forward to meeting in heaven. Of such as these he wrote:

> As for my friends, they are not lost;
> The several vessels of Thy fleet
> Though parted now, by tempests tost,
> Shall safely in the haven meet.

What a homecoming it will be! And how ecumenical! Let ministers prepare the saints as thoroughly for the heavenly banquet as they do for an earthly wedding.[6]

I hope that the examples I have given will suffice to show the importance of equipping the saints for their ministries within and without the church. Taking my cue from what church members have said to me over the years, I have specified some of the things that they say they wish to know. In other words, I have been writing about content. Some, at the present time, wish us to pay particular attention to the context in which we find ourselves; but we need to ponder the term "context". In the deepest sense our context as Christians is life within the orbit of the triune God. Our life, thinking and witness are to be reflective of, as they are sustained by, God's grace and mercy. Often when people think of context they have in mind the particular circumstances in which we are set, and of course we cannot communicate effectively if we pay no heed to these. The church through the ages has been well aware of this, and one might even argue that a lively grasp of that part of the content of theological education which concerns the history of Christian thought and mission through the centuries is precisely the evidence which spares the phrase "theological education is contextual" from being an empty slogan. However, the word "context" in this sense is an elastic term, embracing as it does home, local church, local community, region, nation, world! My main point, however, is that because of the first sense of "context," context in the second sense cannot give us all of our content. We have received a word from God which no earthly context could by itself have provided. It is a gospel word to be addressed to all contexts in all ages, and although we can do no other than receive and interpret it in the context in which we are placed and of which we are inescapably a part (hence the differing accents in which the good news has

6. See further, Sell, *Confessing the Faith Yesterday and Today*, ch. 10.

been proclaimed through the ages and is being proclaimed today), the fact remains that we are, by grace, recipients of revelation, not devisers of a theory constructed by ourselves out of ingredients supplied by our physical or intellectual environment.[7]

It goes without saying that I am not suggesting that ministers simply prime themselves with answers to the above concerns and then mechanically offload them onto the unsuspecting saints in the hope that they will be equally automatically received and later spewed forth. The secret of the theological education of all the saints is to encourage thought, not simply to prime the pumps of memory for the work of uncritical regurgitation. Over a century ago, in a sermon preached before the University of Oxford, J. R. Illingworth made a point that would seem to have continuing relevance: "modern education is increasingly utilitarian. It aims more than heretofore at providing the mind with such definite kinds of information as are likely to be of immediate use in after life, or even in the still nearer future of an examination. . . . [I]t has one grave defect. It trains the receptive rather than the active capabilities of the mind; it teaches men to know rather than to think, and results in a type of intellect that is well-informed, but weak."[8] Principal A. M. Fairbairn had the right idea: "Two things I have laboured to be, the hardest student in my own college, and to sit as a learner among my own men; to study with them, and to encourage them to ask questions which neither they nor I might be able to answer, but which they were the better for stating, while I was not the worse for hearing a problem stated that I could not solve."[9]

## THE EDUCATION OF MINISTERS OF THE GOSPEL

It is as important today as it ever was that ministers take their educational role seriously. William Cowper's plea to the Church of England bishops is susceptible to wider ecumenical interpretation:

> O ye mitred heads,
> Preserve the Church! and lay not careless hands

---

7. For some pertinent reflections see Stackhouse, "Contextualization and Theological Education," See also Sell, *Aspects of Christian Integrity*, 12–14.

8. Illingworth, *University and Cathedral Sermons*, 146–47.

9 Fairbairn, "Experience in Theology," 569.

On skulls that cannot teach, and will not learn.[10]

I emphasise the urgency of the teaching role of the minister of the gospel not least because of the ever thinner spread of ministers of the gospel around and within our pastorates. It would seem that our ministers will need increasingly to serve as resource persons to those within particular churches who will, we may hope, apply their talents with enthusiasm to the strengthening of the fellowship of gathered saints with whom they regularly meet. If ministers are to undertake the necessary task of educating the flock(s) in their care, how are they themselves to be prepared not only for this, but for their liturgical, homiletic and pastoral work as well? What should be the content of the theological education of ministers of the gospel? How, and to whom, is it to be provided?

Our Puritan forebears, taking their cue from Calvin's Geneva Academy, stood for a learned ministry, and by this they meant, above all, a ministry learned in the things of God. But this quite proper focus did not divert them from offering the most thorough education they could to those destined for the ministry of the gospel. In many cases efforts have been made to match the curriculum to the needs and interests of the students and of the churches they would serve. This objective has been achieved in a variety of ways. Over the past 350 years people have come into our ministry by differing routes, and within our formal educational institutions both the overall objectives and, correspondingly, the content of courses has varied significantly over time. The slightest glance at the history of the traditions that have come together in The United Reformed Church will show that it has never been the case that, where ministerial education is concerned, "one size fits all."

## DISSENTING ACADEMIES
## AND THEOLOGICAL COLLEGES

Between 1660 and 1662—the year of the Act of Uniformity, some 2000 ministers resigned, or were ejected from, their Church of England livings, thereby swelling the ranks of those Dissenters who had not taken positions from which they could be removed. Among the points at issue was the legal requirement that the ministers give their "unfeigned assent and consent" to the *Book of Common Prayer* and undertake to use it only in worship. For a

10. Cowper, "The Task," lines 392–94.

variety of reasons—among them the conviction that it was not the preroga-
tive of monarch or parliament to prescribe the worship of the church—those
ejected could not in conscience do this, and hence they forfeited their livings.
Religious tests were imposed by the universities of Oxford and Cambridge,
and with these Dissenting people could not comply. Accordingly, with a view
to providing a higher education for their young men they began to establish
Dissenting academies in many parts of the country.

By the end of the eighteenth century more than seventy academies had
been opened; they varied in size and some were short-lived. The tutors of
the earliest academies had been schooled at Oxford or Cambridge, among
them John Woodhouse, who had studied at Trinity College Cambridge and
conducted his academy at Sheriffhales from 1676 to 1697; Matthew Warren
of St. John's College Oxford, who superintended Taunton Academy from
1687 until his death in 1706; and Richard Frankland, an alumnus of Christ's
College Cambridge, whose academy, founded at Rathmell in 1670, was
forced to remove on four occasions until the Toleration Act of 1689 made
it possible for a return to the original location. The list of subjects taught at
Sheriffhales is as follows: mathematics, natural philosophy, logic, rhetoric,
metaphysics, ethics, geography, history, anatomy, law, natural theology,
doctrine, Hebrew, and Greek. This list is not untypical of that in other academies, and it makes clear that students destined for non-ministerial careers
were in view no less than candidates for ordination. The instruction was
given through the medium of Latin, and a significant proportion of the set
texts were in that language. It is quite remarkable that despite the provoca-
tions he endured, Richard Frankland educated 304 students in all.

Whereas Woodhouse, Warren, and Frankland were Presbyterians,
Theophilus Gale, of Magdalen College Oxford, was a Congregationalist.
He opened Newington Green Academy *circa* 1666 and was succeeded by
Thomas Rowe in 1678, Among Rowe's students were the Congregationalist
Isaac Watts, who composed an ode in Rowe's honour, and the Presbyterian Henry Grove. In all of this we have an indication of the denominational fluidity of the times and, in Grove's case, of family connections; for
Rowe, who became tutor at the age of twenty-one, was his cousin. Grove
succeeded Warren at Taunton Academy, where he was in turn succeeded
by his nephew and student, Thomas Amory. Among the more important
academies of the eighteenth century was that of Philip Doddridge, opened
in Kibworth in 1729 and removed with Doddridge to Northampton later
the same year. Doddridge broke with tradition in teaching through the

medium of English, and in this he was followed by Caleb Ashworth, his student who, in accordance with Doddridge's wishes, assumed charge of the Academy when it removed to Daventry on Doddridge's death in 1752.

With the Evangelical Revival of the eighteenth century academies specifically devoted to the preparation of ministers began to appear. Among these was that opened in 1783 at Newport Pagnell by William Bull, who had been educated under Ashworth at Daventry. The evangelical thrust of the enterprise is suggested by the fact that Bull sought advice as to a desirable curriculum from his friend the evangelical Anglican, John Newton. Newton emphasized the importance of basing all instruction on the Bible, and warned Bull of such things as metaphysics and philosophy, which could be hurtful to the faith. Under the bovine succession of William, Thomas P., and Josiah Bull, the academy, which served both Congregational and Baptist students, survived until 1853. Those Newport Pagnell students whose course was not completed were transferred to Cheshunt College. The origins of this College lay in the Countess of Huntingdon's College at Trevecca, Breconshire. Established there in 1768, it removed to Hertfordshire, its Trust Deed of 1792 stipulating that while relations with the Countess's Connexion would be maintained, the institution was to be evangelical, not narrowly denominational. A further removal took the College to Cambridge in 1905, and to eventual association with the Presbyterian Westminster College in 1967.

That the older idea of the Dissenting academy with a broad curriculum did more than linger is shown by the fact that in on 14 September 1786, three years after the foundation of the evangelical Newport Pagnell Academy, Thomas Barnes, on the occasion of the opening of the theologically liberal Manchester Academy, spoke thus: "Of all subjects, Divinity seems most to demand the aid of kindred, and even of apparently remoter sciences. Its objects are God and Man: and nothing, which can either illustrate the perfections of the one, or the nature, capacities, and history of the other, can be entirely unimportant."[11] He proceeded to list the following subjects as among those to which attention needed to be paid: natural philosophy, natural history, chemistry, anatomy and physiology, history, and languages. All of these, he thought, contributed towards "forming the accomplished and useful Minister of Religion."[12] True to the academy heritage, he did not

11. Barnes, *A Discourse delivered at the Commencement of the Manchester Academy*, 14.

12. Ibid., 14.

stop there, but turned his attention to the other learned professions and their needs, to those destined to civil and commercial life; and he wondered why the "man of trade" should be "doomed to ignorance and insipidity," and why such persons might not be elevated above "mercantile drudgery."[13] The sponsors of the Academy even envisaged the appointment of professors of mathematics and natural philosophy, and teachers of French, Italian, drawing, writing, arithmetic, and merchants accounts.[14]

In other parts of the country Congregational theological colleges mushroomed. The heritage of New College, London, more completely spans the line from Dissenting academies to Revival-inspired theological colleges than any other: the types of institution are clearly identifiable from their names, and I group them by way of showing the three streams which came together in 1850 to form New College, London, and the distinct line which resulted in the union of New with Hackney College in 1924:

a. The King's Head Society (1730–1817); The Homerton Academy (1817–23); Homerton College (1823–50).

b. Northampton Academy (1729–51 and 1789–99); Daventry Academy (1752–89); Wymondley Academy (1799–1833); Coward College (1833–50).

c. Hoxton Academy (1788–1826); Highbury College (1826–50).

d. New College, London (1850–1924).

e. The Village Itinerancy Society (1796–1839); Hackney Theological Seminary (1839–71); Hackney College (1871–1924).

*Hackney and New College* (1924). The College was re-named New College, London in 1936. It closed in 1977.

In the South West a college was opened at Ottery St. Mary in 1752. In 1765 it migrated to Bridport, where it remained until it moved to Taunton in 1780. It proceeded to Axminster in 1795, and to Exeter in 1829. From 1845 it continued in Plymouth, where it united with the Bristol Theological Institute (1863) in 1891. Its final manifestation was as The Western College, Bristol (1901–69). Yorkshire United Independent College, Bradford, was the successor of colleges at Heckmondwike (1756). Northowram (1783), Rotherham (1795), Idle (1800), and Airedale (1826). It was the product of the union of Airedale with Rotherham in 1888, and it continued until

13. Ibid. 23.

14. Ibid., Appendix, 4–5.

its union with Lancashire Independent College in 1958. The latter college (1843–1958) had Roby's Academy (1803–8), Leaf Square Academy, Pendleton (1811–13) and Blackburn Academy (1816) in its lineage. In 1968 Paton College, Nottingham (1920–68)—the predecessors of which were Cavendish College, Manchester (1860–63) and the Nottingham Congregational Institute (1863–1920)—removed to Manchester and became part of the union of colleges there. It should be noted that the origins of Paton College lay in a sense of mission to the then burgeoning industrial towns and cities, and that throughout its existence it made special provision for older ministerial candidates.[15] Finally, in 1969, Western College likewise made the move to Manchester.

A significant number of Congregational and United Reformed ministers received their theological education in Wales. The roots of the Presbyterian College, Carmarthen, which was open to Protestant Dissenters in general, reach down to the academy opened at Brynllywarch in 1689 by Samuel Jones. It subsequently sojourned in a number of locations, but was continuously in Carmarthen from 1796 until 1979, when it removed to Swansea in cooperation with Memorial College, which had itself moved there from Brecon in 1959. From 1980 onwards both institutions were based in Aberystwyth where, together with the United Theological College of the Presbyterian Church of Wales, they were members of the Aberystwyth and Lampeter School of Theology of the University of Wales. In 1757 the Congregationalists, suspicious of liberal theological tendencies in the Carmarthen Presbyterian College (the emphasis of which increasingly became Unitarian), established an academy at Abergavenny. It removed first to Wrexham, then to Llanfyllin and Newtown, and arrived in Brecon in 1837, where it remained until 1959, as we have seen. Finally, in 1841 a theological college was opened at Llanuwchllyn, which removed to Bala in the following year. Friction over constitutional matters led to the establishment of another college in Bangor. Peace having eventually broken out, the Bala College removed to the larger centre of Bangor, and the institution was thenceforth known as Bala-Bangor Independent College. It closed in 1989 and, like Brecon College before it, transferred its work to Aberystwyth.

---

15. I have never been able to bring myself to speak of "mature" students when thinking of those over the age of twenty-five. There is no necessary connection between psychological maturity and chronological age. I have met some very mature eighteen-year-olds and some innocents abroad who were in their fifties. Hence my practice of referring when necessary to "older" students.

Students for the ministry of the Union of Welsh Independents were also educated at the institutions just described.

In 1831 the Congregationalists opened a theological college at Spring Hill, Birmingham—a rapidly-growing and staunchly Nonconformist town. Henry Rogers and Richard Alliott taught there; the college's best-known alumnus was undoubtedly R. W. Dale; and David Worthington Simon was its last principal, for in 1886 the college removed to Oxford as Mansfield College. Simon proceeded to Edinburgh as principal of the Scottish Congregational College, while A. M. Fairbairn left Airedale College to become the first principal of the first Nonconformist College to settle in Oxford—the realization of an ambition that had been nurtured by the removal in 1871 of religious tests at Oxford and Cambridge Universities. Under the leadership of John Marsh and others Mansfield College became a permanent private hall of the University in 1955, and forty years later it became a full college of the University. It ceased to undertake ministerial training in 2007.

Three theological colleges that belong to the heritage of The United Reformed Church remain to be mentioned at this juncture, those of the Congregational Union of Scotland, the Presbyterian Church of England and the Churches of Christ. The first teachers of the Glasgow Theological Academy (1812), Greville Ewing and Ralph Wardlaw provided theological education for Scottish Congregational ordinands whilst continuing in pastoral charge themselves. In 1855 the college removed to Edinburgh under W. L. Alexander, and from 1921 was known as the Scottish Congregational College. In 1930 it was joined by the United Free Church College. Principals flowed across the Scottish border in both directions, with the Lancashire College alumni D. W. Simon and J. M. Hodgson, the Welsh New College alumnus, Thomas Hywel Hughes, and P. T. Forsyth's student, H. F. Lovell Cocks, going north, and Charles S. Duthie, who had earlier served as tutor at Paton College, moving south to be the last principal of New College, London. The majority of Scottish Congregationalists united with The United Reformed Church in 2000.

As already indicated, by the end of the first two decades of the nineteenth century most of the Presbyterian churches of Old Dissent had become Congregational, while a significant number of them had become Unitarian. A remnant of trinitarian Presbyterian churches was left, most of them in North East England. They united with members of the Church of Scotland who settled in England from 1707 onwards, and eventually the

Presbyterian Church *in* England was constituted. This Church united with the United Presbyterian churches on English soil to form the Presbyterian Church *of* England in 1876. Meanwhile the Presbyterian Church *in* England, which sided with Scotland's Free Church at the Disruption of 1843, had opened its Theological College in London in 1844, with a Principal and professors all drawn from the Free Church of Scotland. In 1899 the institution removed to Cambridge, took the name Westminster College, and continues thus to this day. Its ability to attract a galaxy of scholarly talent to its staff is epitomized by the fact that John Skinner, C. A. Anderson Scott, John Oman and P. Carnegie Simpson overlapped as colleagues there from 1914 to 1922. Unlike all the other academies and colleges I have mentioned, this college, in both its London and Cambridge expressions, has from the outset been owned first by the Presbyterian Church *in* (from 1876, *of*) England and now by The United Reformed Church.

From the 1850s onwards the question of the training of evangelists was raised among the Churches of Christ, and some attempts were made to meet this need. But, no less than in some Congregational, Baptist and Methodist, quarters, there were those who took determined exception to the notion of formal, college, theological education. Among these was David King, who had presided over the Liverpool Conference of 1878. Others were more favourably disposed to the idea, among them John M'Cartney, President in 1912, who had been involved with the denomination's correspondence courses since 1896, in which year their originator, Alexander Brown, died. Eventually Overdale College was opened in Birmingham in 1920, under the principalship of William Robinson, though from this it should not be inferred that all would now be sweetness and light. On the contrary, in 1923 there was friction over Robinson's desire to affiliate the College with the Student Christian Movement, and three years later with the teaching of the tutor Joseph Smith. In both cases the motivating anxiety was that a drift in the direction of theological liberalism was occurring. In 1931 the College moved from its Moseley premises to Selly Oak, where it joined other colleges in an ecumenical environment, and where Robinson served until 1951. The College closed *circa* 1980, and the Re-formed Association of Churches of Christ united with The United Reformed Church in 1981.[16]

It remains to add that a number of ministers—especially accessions to the Presbyterian Church of England from Scotland, Ireland and

16. For a fuller account, to which I am indebted, see Thompson, *Let Sects and Parties Fall*, 67–71, 130–34.

Wales—were educated in other parts of the United Kingdom; that some have transferred from other such other denominations as the Church of England, the Wesleyan Reform Union, the Baptist Union, and the Salvation Army; and that a number have been added to the ministerial roll of The United Reformed Church who were educated elsewhere in the world. Finally, some ministers have been educated at independent Bible and evangelical colleges, among them some of the fifty-one Congregationalists who were trained at Harley College from its foundation in 1878 to its closure in 1915. This evangelical interdenominational college was founded by Henry Grattan Guinness of the Bibles (as distinct from the beers) side of that comfortably placed family. He had been accepted for training at New College, but evangelistic demands upon his time inundated him, and he left before completing his course. Among other things he opened in Dublin a Bible school for evangelists, and this was the forerunner of Harley College, for which his son, Harry Grattan Guinness, took responsibility, and which ceased with his death.[17] Many of the College's alumni served with the Regions Beyond Missionary Union.

## FROM "GIFTED BRETHREN" TO CONGREGATIONAL UNION EXAMINATIONS

It is entirely conceivable that over the past 350 years half of those in pastoral charge of churches of the four traditions which have coalesced in The United Reformed Church had no college education at all. Figures, especially for the earlier centuries, are difficult to compute because under Congregational polity in particular, it was possible for a local church to call ministers regardless of educational considerations. Indeed, in earlier times "gifted brethren" might be raised up within a church and in due course be called to serve as minister; or they might be despatched to other needy churches, or to plant new causes. Many were regarded as lay pastors, some of them "tent-makers," and without them many smaller churches would have been deprived of pastoral leadership altogether. There were, of course, unfortunate possibilities in all of this. Odd ideas might be promulgated from the pulpit; domineering personalities might regard the pastorate as a personal bailiwick (though, truth to tell, a college education was not an infallible preservative against either of these misfortunes). But with the passage of time, and with the impetus to mission supplied by the Evangelical Revival and

17. See further, Sell, *Commemorations*, ch. 12.

the rise of the modern missionary movement, it was increasingly felt that the needs of the villages—and not only they—were such that a more determined and coherent effort of evangelism and church planting was required. This, in turn, led to the realization that if such efforts were to be supported by subscription, the organizing bodies ought to have some responsibility for those who were working in their name, and that the evangelists and pastors ought to be held accountable for their labours—or lack of them. It is not difficult to imagine that such possibilities would frequently be regarded as unwarrantable meddling by Congregationalists of an isolationist turn of mind—if such are conceivable.

There are many gaps in the story of non-college-educated ministers, some of which may never be filled; but it is possible to indicate some of the steps which led to the situation which prevailed until 1972. At the turn of the eighteenth century, and under the continuing inspiration of the Evangelical Revival, Congregationalists were becoming involved in more inter-denominational ventures than ever before, among them the Religious Tract Society (1799), and the British and Foreign Bible Society (1804). The London Missionary Society (1795) was becoming well established. The thoughts of some began increasingly to turn to mission at home. James Bowden, minister at Tooting, was concerned that while Christians were going to the ends of the earth with the gospel, there was a sizeable untapped mission field populated by villages, many of which were utterly deprived of the gospel. He called a group of likeminded Christians together and in 1797 the Surrey Mission was founded. It was not exclusively a Congregational venture, for Baptists and others were welcome to participate; but without question the Mission served the county's Congregationalism well, as did similar societies in other counties. In 1836 there were said to be 994 churches and 579 Home Mission Stations in thirty-nine county Associations.[18] Three years later, at the first Autumn Assembly of the Congregational Union of England and Wales, a plan for the evangelization of the whole country was discussed. Among the objectives were those of combating religious ignorance, proclaiming the gospel, and working for the conversion of sinners. It was resolved that the Union would undertake this work in conjunction with confederated churches and Associations, "That lay agency be employed under the superintendence of churches and pastors, but that ministerial missionaries be invariably educated. That energetic evangelists

18. A. Peel, *These Hundred Years*, 102.

be sought out and employed."[19] By 1840 the Home Missionary Society had 120 missionaries, and concern was expressed that some college students eschewed the work because they felt that traditional pastorates were "more respectable and comfortable."[20] A further challenge was the rise of "Puseyite" clergy who denied the credentials of Congregational ministers, accused home missionaries of "breaking into Christ's fold," and insisted that only those men who had been ordained in the apostolic succession (as they understood it) had the right to preach the gospel.[21]

As early as 1845 the question of the propriety of funding evangelists of doubtful character was raised. It was not denied that a local church had the right to call whom it would, but the Union felt under no obligation to supply funds in doubtful cases. Gradually the Congregational Union assumed ever greater control over the organization of home missionary work. The question of un- or inadequately educated ministers was, by the turn of the nineteenth century, deemed by many to require urgent resolution. In 1901 D. W. Simon published a letter in which he observed that of 3,123 Congregational ministers, 692 had not received a college education,[22] and shortly "Rules relating to the Recognition of Churches and Ministers" were adopted. It was resolved that evangelists and lay pastors without college training who were called to pastorates must show evidence of good character and receive in-service training. In due course those who were successful in the examinations found themselves on a ministerial List B (they were "recognized" but not ordained), and it became possible for them to undertake further study whilst continuing in their pastorates, with a view to becoming fully accredited ministers on List A, with all that that meant in terms of more secure stipends and pensions. Eventually the surviving List B ministers were promoted to List A by the Ministerial Status Committee, and thus ended a two-tier ministry which, within Congregationalism, had never been justifiable in theological terms.[23] Since I shall shortly be arguing the need for more scholar-pastors I must preempt the possible charge of snobbish elitism by testifying that of the three ministers who influenced me most, one had been trained at Harley College, one was a Lancashire College

---

19. Ibid., 115.

20. Ibid., 151.

21. Ibid., 152.

22. Simon, "The Congregational Ministry in the British Isles," 374 (but misprinted as 274).

23. See further, Sell, "The Unsung Ministers of Congregationalism's List B."

educated non-graduate, and the third came through List B. There could not have been more captivating preachers or devoted pastors.

## THE COLLEGES AND THE UNIVERSITIES

What were the objectives of those who founded or supported our modern denominational theological colleges? They had certain common aspirations, but also some particular motivations. Among the latter, for example, was the concern of Lancastrian Congregationalists that Unitarianism was well-established in the county, whereas over the Pennines in Yorkshire the heterodox had not made so much headway. This was attributed to the fact that Yorkshire was supplied with Congregational theological colleges, whereas Lancashire was not. Not to be outdone (shades of the Wars of the Roses), and the short-lived Roby's and Leaf Square academies having ceased, the Lancastrians resolved upon establishing a more permanent academy in Blackburn. During the annual meeting of the friends of Blackburn Independent Academy held on 23 and 24 June 1818 William Roby delivered a sermon entitled, "Academical Institutions; or the Importance of Preparatory Instruction for the Christian Ministry." His text was Ephesians 4:11–12, from which the phrase "for the work of ministry" later became the motto of Lancashire Independent College. Roby applied a modicum of homiletic embroidery to verse 12, and understood it to mean that Christ appointed apostles, prophets, evangelists, pastors and teachers "For the adaptation, or preparatory instruction of holy men for the ministry, in order to the edifying of the body of Christ."[24] From this he drew his three points:

> First, That the ministry of the gospel is divinely intended to be continued as a *standing ordinance* in the church of Christ. Secondly, That the persons employed in the work of the Christian ministry ought to be *saints*, or holy men. . . . Thirdly, That persons intended for the ministry of the gospel ought to be adapted to the work by *preparatory instruction*. Literature, the most general, and the most profound, cannot possibly supply the want of sanctity; and sanctity itself, without a competent measure of knowledge, leaves a person unqualified for ministerial service.[25]

Roby went on to remind his hearers that Jesus himself did not send forth his apostles until they had been under his tutelage for three years.

24. Slate, *A Brief History*, 122.

25. Ibid., 123.

In 1843 we find Robert Vaughan, like Baxter before him and Fairbairn after him, largely self-taught, declaiming in his inaugural lecture as the first President of Lancashire Independent College that

> The design of this institute is, the education of students with a view to the Christian ministry. Its benefits shall be restricted to persons whose piety shall be beyond doubt. To such persons it will extend the advantages of mental discipline and learning, together with the cultivation of the kind of ability especially required in the discharge of the duties of the preacher and the pastor in the churches of our order.[26]

Ever keen to demonstrate to the genteel classes that they need not fear Nonconformity, Vaughan's "solemn conviction" was that "it is not so much the doctrines we preach, and the manner of our preaching, which renders our ministry so little acceptable to a large portion of the educated classes of society."[27]

In a quite different style Henry Forster Burder, in his address at the opening of Highbury College spoke with urgency about a tide of unbelief which was sweeping the world, which only a particular kind of theological curriculum could stop in its tracks:

> Can the friends of our theological seminaries be insensible to the daring character of that philosophy, falsely so called, which sets itself with determined hostility against the religion of the Bible? Has it not taken possession of the continent of Europe, of many of the seats of learning, and even of many designated by the name of theology, in its various and important branches? By its insidious predilections from the academic chair, and its sceptical effusions through the medium of the press, has it not ventured to impugn, and endeavoured to subvert, the most glorious truths of the Christian faith?

Hence Burder's quest of a curriculum in which the energies of the mind were subjugated "to the supreme and controlling authority of the dictates of divine revelation."[28]

From the middle of the nineteenth century onwards the question of the theological education of ministers of the gospel was increasingly raised from the point of view of the most appropriate curriculum. There were still

26. Vaughan, *Protestant Nonconformity in its Relation to Learning and Piety*, 44.

27. Ibid., 50.

28. Burder, "The Objects and Progress of the Institution," 33–34.

some who viewed formal theological education as a plague to be avoided at all costs, and it would be interesting to know whether any of that persuasion expressed their mind to A. M. Fairbairn. There can be no doubt as to what his reaction would have been, for in an ordination sermon he thundered,

> If ever there was an insane and disastrous delusion it is the delusion that an imperfectly educated man is good enough to preach the Gospel. . . . Providence has now and then made an undisciplined man a great preacher; its ordinary rule is to bestow gifts where they have been bravely earned by patient discipline and toil. Tax your brains. Brains never die of work. They die of inertia.[29]

But what should be taught? A few soundings in chronological order will suggest the answer. The curriculum at Blackburn Independent Academy (1816) comprised Latin, Greek, the biblical oriental languages, history, geography, mathematics, natural philosophy, the theory of languages and general grammar, mental philosophy, theology, and ecclesiastical history.[30] Against any who might think otherwise, the American, E. N. Kirk, in the course of his lecture of 4 July 1839 at Cheshunt College, waxed lyrical over Greek and Hebrew: "The Hebrew and Greek Scriptures ought to become the familiar companions of a Gospel minister. There is a sweetness, unction, and power in them, which can be felt, but not translated."[31] The possibility evidently did not occur to him that any had been embittered, numbed and weakened by linguistic toil. But it was not long before J. Frost, while not doubting the importance of mathematics and the classical languages, was wondering whether, in view of the differing ages and abilities of ministerial candidates, they were essential to preachers of the gospel.[32]

A more general stimulus to curriculum revision was provided when the University of London, at the time an examining body, held its first examinations in Arts in 1839,[33] and when secular colleges of higher education,

29. Quoted by Grieve, "Christian Learning and Christian Living," 81.

30. Slate, *A Brief History*, 126.

31. Kirk, *The Obligations of the Church to secure a Learned and Pious Ministry*, 13. For a more recent, powerful defence of the biblical languages see Harman, "The Place of the Biblical Languages in the Theological Curriculum."

32. Frost, "The Expediency of a Seminary in which only an English Theological Education should be Given," 22–23.

33. By 1850 119 degrees (MA 16, BA, 98, LLB, 5) out of 489 degrees had been awarded to students entered through Congregational colleges. So Grieve, "A Hundred Years of Ministerial Training," 261. Robert Vaughan, the first, and Henry Rogers, the second President of Lancashire Independent College had been professors in London University.

which in time developed into fully-fledged universities, were established in growing cities. From the point of view of ministerial education, Owens College, founded in Manchester in 1851 is of particular importance, for it enabled an amendment to the curriculum of Lancashire College such that Arts subjects were be taken at Owens, thereby enabling the Congregational professors to concentrate upon the theological disciplines. They could thus participate in the Senatus Academicus, a consortium of theological colleges established in 1879. The idea had been broached by H. R. Reynolds, president of Cheshunt College, at a conference of delegates of Congregational colleges as far back as 1865. Echoing H. F. Burder, he challenged his colleagues thus: "The controversies which are closing round the Church, and engaging the most active minds in the Europe of this generation, in a war to the knife with our holy Christianity, demand that we, as well as other sections of the Church, should furnish our contingent to the great army, which is prepared to fight the battle for the truth as it is in Jesus Christ."[34]

Two qualifications were offered by the Senatus: the Associateship and the Fellowship, the former being of the standard of a postgraduate divinity degree, the latter, of an earned Master's degree.[35] By 1885, eight Congregational colleges, the London Presbyterian College, and two Baptist colleges were members of the Senatus; by 1901 membership had risen to seventeen comprising the Presbyterian College, now in Cambridge and re-named Westminster, seven Baptist colleges, and nine Congregational colleges including the Congregational College of Victoria, Melbourne. Distinguished examiners were appointed—119 of them over the entire period—among them Robert Adamson, Edward Caird, Marcus Dods, Robert Flint, James Iverach, J. H. Moulton and James Orr. The examinations were rigorous, and the instruction to point passages of Hebrew was not overlooked. Between 1880 and 1901 511 candidates gained the ATS, and 11 the FTS.[36]

The demise of the Senatus was brought about by the provision of theological studies in the reconstituted University of London (1900), with which a number of Senatus member colleges became associated; and by the foundation of Faculties of Theology in Manchester and Wales, and later in other

---

34. *Minutes of the Proceedings of a Conference of Delegates*, 42.

35. "Earned" to distinguish it from the MAs of the ancient Scottish universities, where the MA was a first degree; and from the MAs of Oxford and Cambridge, which required no further academic study.

36. See further on the Senatus, Sell, *Philosophy, Dissent and Nonconformity*, 128–32; and the *Reports* of the Senatus for 1885 and 1901, which were published in London in those years for the Senatus.

civic universities. Fairbairn was prominent in urging that formal theological study should be undertaken by postgraduates, who would ideally build it upon an Arts degree. This plan he had introduced from the outset on arrival at Mansfield College; but he also commended it far and wide, not least to those in the University of Wales who were contemplating the introduction of a Bachelor of Divinity degree. He was also, together with the Anglican William Sanday, an adviser to those contemplating the inauguration of a Faculty of Theology at Manchester and, true to his convictions, he strongly advocated the provision of a postgraduate BD, in contrast to that of London University, where the BD was, and remains, a first degree. Fairbairn's view prevailed, and the Manchester Faculty was inaugurated in 1904. It was the first freestanding non-confessional Faculty in the land, and it opened its theological degrees to women from the outset. It pioneered (and made compulsory) the study of Comparative Religion, and Hebrew and Greek likewise could not be avoided. The philosophy and psychology of religion, biblical studies, ecclesiastical history, and, later, Christian ethics were also taught. Out of respect for those with sensitive doctrinal antennae, the history of Christian doctrine was taught in the theological colleges, as were some of the University certificate classes. Provision was made not only for the BD, but for the DD, obtainable on the successful submission of published works deemed to have made a distinguished and original contribution to learning. The DD was not earned until 1920,[37] and it has been only very sparingly awarded since. Students who graduated with first or upper second class honours in Arts, or with the combination BA, BD, could proceed to the MA by thesis. The founding staff of the Faculty comprised three appointed by the University, among them the Primitive Methodist A. S. Peake and many drawn from the eight[38] theological colleges in the city, among them the Congregationalists W. F. Adeney and Robert Mackintosh.[39] By 1920, when the centenary, delayed by War, of Blackburn Independent Academy was celebrated, Principal W. H. Bennett could say,

37. The degree has occasionally been awarded as an honorary degree—to A. M. Fairbairn, for example, who was similarly honoured by the University of Wales, among others.

38. Didsbury Wesleyan College (1834), Lancashire Independent College (1843), Manchester Unitarian College (1854), Victoria Park United Methodist Church College (1871), The Moravian College (1877), Hartley Primitive Methodist College (1881), Manchester Baptist College (1887), and the Anglican Training College (1889).

39. See further, Sell, *The Theological Education of the Ministry*, ch. 8.

Nearly all the Arts classes and a large proportion of the Theological classes are taken at the University with University lecturers and professors. The College is thus able to use a large staff of distinguished teachers, and need only maintain a limited staff of its own. On the other hand, the theological staff of our College—the Principal and Dr. [Robert] Mackintosh—are recognised as Lecturers of the University, and their classes are reckoned as University classes which are open to all students of the University.[40]

Sufficient has been said to show that ministers came into the traditions which flowed into The United Reformed Church, and into that Church itself, by a variety of routes. In summary: there were the Dissenting academies which provided a higher education to male students destined for a variety of professions; they were overlapped and then succeeded by theological colleges founded specifically for the education of ministers; in due course some of these colleges entered students for Arts degrees of the University of London and Owens College, Manchester; a significant number of colleges joined the Theological Senatus, which provided degree-level examinations in theology; with the removal of doctrinal tests at Oxford and Cambridge, the advent of the University of London's Faculty of Divinity, and with the founding of modern universities, notably in the first instance, Manchester, close, but not identical, relationships with universities became possible, with attendant curriculum implications; the Presbyterian foundation, Westminster College, a partner in the Theological Senatus, brought a distinctive and distinguished heritage into The United Reformed Church, and now takes its place within the Cambridge Federation of Theological Colleges; and further gifts have come to The United Reformed Church through Overdale College of the Churches of Christ, and through the emphasis within that tradition upon the ministry of elders. Ministers have been educated in other parts of the United Kingdom—especially at the Scottish Congregational College which, since the union of 2000, makes its home within The United Reformed Church; in independent colleges, and in other parts of the world. A significant number of ministers have had no college education, but were lay pastors, or home missionaries or evangelists who, in later years, were able to proceed by Congregational Union examinations to List B and thence, if they wished, by further examination to List A, the list of fully accredited Congregational ministers. Most recently,

---

40. Quoted in *Centenary of the Lancashire Independent College, 1816–1916, celebrated 1920*, 11.

some ministers have been trained at the ecumenical Queens College Birmingham, and, especially for non-stipendiary ministry, through extension courses, and on a part-time basis at regional ecumenical centres.

## THE CURRICULUM ACTUAL AND DESIRABLE

The first point to grasp is that no theological course can cover all that ministers might need to know at some point during their ministries. On this point two of our distinguished principals were in complete accord. Following his assumption of the principalship of Westminster College in 1922, John Oman canvassed opinions as to the most appropriate curriculum for intending ministers. The strongest reply came from Woodrow Wilson, the twenty-eighth president of the United States, who had earlier been president of Princeton University: "Stick at all costs to your four central subjects [biblical studies, ecclesiastical history, systematic theology, and practical theology]. Our method means utterly superficial knowledge."[41] Robert Franks of Western College agreed. In his annual report to the subscribers for 1926 he wrote, "It is too often forgotten that the ideal of ministerial education is not to send a man out with some knowledge of every subject he will afterwards find useful. It is to send him out with a mind that can tackle with success any subject as need arises. The opposite leads to self-confident shallowness."[42]

However unfashionable it may, in some quarters, seem to be, I suggest that there is much wisdom in these judgments. First, well-nigh omniscient though some of them have pretended to be, it is asking too much of theological educators to provide whatever knowledge may be useful to a minister three or four decades hence. But ministers who have mastered what was provided, and whose minds have not ossified, will be able to absorb what is useful, and adversely criticize what is not, from whatever quarter it comes. Secondly, the position adopted by Oman and Franks rightly implies that the theological education of ministers of the gospel (and, of course, genuine education at large) has to do with more than the pragmatic supply of "tricks for the trade". (Why do even university people write as if they think that the only reason for learning Spanish is that graduates may speak intelligently to Latin American business magnates?) Thirdly, Oman

41. Typescript "Memorandum" addressed to the Moderator's committee on the ministry.

42. Western College Minute Book.

and Franks were spared what has sometimes been called "the tyranny of modules." These are courses of normally eight to twelve weeks' duration which, when compounded and satisfactorily completed, yield a degree. The president of a well-known American seminary proudly informed me that his students could choose from more than 200 course options. Without rigorous scrutiny by a dean of studies this can mean that students pick from the smorgasbord what most appeals to them; it is a wonderful way of avoiding more challenging disciplines, and the resulting degree may have little coherence and, still worse, show little evidence of progression in depth over the total length of the course. It seems odd when in their final year students are still taking courses entitled, "A survey of," or "An introduction to . . . ." Yet again, the very brevity of modules can mean that students do not have time to become truly immersed in the disciplines and thus, by giving them such a small dose all we have done is to inoculate them against the subjects for life. I do not say that coherence and progression cannot be achieved within a modular regime, or that modules have no place in full-time, extension or in-service courses; but where degree courses are concerned, careful organization is needed to ensure that students are guided through a coherent course, and that the pitfalls I have indicated are avoided.

It is also the case that a modular structure can, no less than more traditionally organized courses, play into the hands of those who are so ideologically-minded as to be sectarian in their attitudes. This comes about when people elevate their own experience into a lens through which they seek to construe the whole of theology. We thus find courses on ecumenical theology from which opponents of the World Council of Churches and all its works are absent; liberation theology modules which are taken by Hispanics but not by right-wing whites; courses on feminist theology in which no men—least of misogynists—are to be seen. How is the ideal of cut and thrust of free and open debate, one of the pillars of higher education, to be realized if students can so easily avoid it, and if the very people who need to be faced with what to them are "alien" views are spared the challenge? The only remedy I can see is that the insights of ecumenical, liberation and feminist theology should be introduced into an extended, broad, required course of theology. Then those who so wish could pursue particular topics further and in greater depth, and among them might be some whose appetite for the subject had been whetted during the comprehensive course. The students would then be pursuing their particular interests having seen them in relation to other approaches in theology, and not as if they represented the only worthwhile aspect of that varied discipline.

I now wish to show how, in terms of its curriculum, one of our colleges sought to be faithful to the idea that where ministerial education is concerned, it is not the case that one size fits all. I select Lancashire Independent College because through the University of Manchester its students could take as wide a range of courses as anywhere else in the land. First there was the opportunity of studying for an Arts degree followed by the postgraduate BD. This normally kept students occupied for six years. Secondly there was a one-year Certificate in Biblical Knowledge (introduced in 1906), on which was built the Certificate in Theology (from 1913)—a three or four year course. In 1945 the three-year degree of BA (Theology) was introduced—a hybrid comprising a selection of courses from Arts and Theology, administered by the Faculty of Arts. In addition to the University courses the college offered courses on worship and pastoral theology; and there was the weekly sermon class. There was also a college scheme, inaugurated by A. J. Grieve, which ensured that all students sat examinations on the English text of the Bible on the first and last Saturday of every term. A student who completed six years of training would have been examined on the contents and contexts of all the books of the Bible (not only on the texts in Greek and Hebrew set for the BD, or the texts in English set for the University Certificate). In addition to all of this students were sent all over Lancashire, Cheshire and parts of Yorkshire as itinerant preachers, and some, having been invited to do so by Church Meetings, undertook summer pastorates in vacant churches. Through all of this, and not least through the daily morning and evening prayers in chapel and homespun social activities (not to mention sports-field battles with, and subsequent raids upon, the Methodists and Baptists) ministers were formed.

The regime as described was current from the formation of the Faculty of Theology in 1904 to 1958 when Lancashire College and Yorkshire United College were amalgamated. It is the regime that I underwent, and I remain very grateful for it. I am tempted to reminisce, but I shall resist, and simply state that, owing to the distinguished scholars then in post, I could not have had better schooling in either Arts or Theology.[43] I proceed to some general observations.

---

43. I have written a little more about this in *Philosophy, History and* Theology, 3–4, and in *The Theological Education of the Ministry*, ch. 8.

First, it will not do to view past theological education through rose-tinted spectacles. For a variety of reasons, some candidates did not complete their courses, others resigned early from the ministry of the gospel, and by no means all persisted with disciplined study following ordination. It was ever thus. During his ministry in Dublin (1827–32) James Martineau attended a meeting called to examine candidates for license, and could not help noticing that some of the ministerial inquisitors "sat through the ordeal gravely holding their Hebrew Bibles upside down."[44]

Secondly, I continue to believe that it is for the good of the ministry if some of our ordinands are able to complete both Arts and Divinity degrees. By way of showing that I am not alone in this I summon Joseph Figures, an alumnus of Yorkshire United College, many of whose students read Arts at Edinburgh University (and occasionally at Leeds University) prior to their theological studies. Of the Arts course Figures writes,

> Its value has been not only in the broad and permanent background of culture and knowledge it has supplied, but in the disciplined habits of mind it has produced. It has taught men to read systematically and discriminately over a wide field and to assess the worth of what they have read. It has fostered independence of thought and stimulated the regular companionship of great minds whose wisdom is the inheritance of the ages. It has trained men in qualities of intellectual discernment and competence which, when applied to the practical affairs of the world, are most truly formative of wise judgment and effective action.[45]

Figures was well aware that his case had to be made in face of opposition:

> [W]e have to be on our guard against those who think there are short cuts in the training and work of the ministry, and who emphasise practical experience, insight into affairs or contact with living men and real needs as the means best adapted to produce efficient and wise judgment. . . . There are those today who would shorten the period of ministerial training and minimise the importance of traditional culture and learning. . . . But there are indications in the ministry today, as in other walks of life also, that there are already far too many with little more to offer to the world and its needs than the ragged edges of half-knowledge and incomplete education.

44. McLachlan, *Essays and Addresses*, 181.
45. Figures, "The Value of a Liberal Education," 34.

As a provincial moderator[46] and sometime Chairman of the Congregational Union of England and Wales, Figures knew of what he spoke. The fact that his words were written more than half a century ago in no way invalidates the point he makes. It does, however, suggest that with fewer young candidates than hitherto, and in the absence of the grants that used to be available at least for first degrees, we must redouble our efforts to ensure that academically able young candidates receive the support they need to utilise their gifts and fulfil their vocation.

Thirdly, it must be acknowledged that it was only ever a minority of ministers who achieved an Arts degree and a postgraduate Divinity degree. From the founding of Manchester's Faculty of Theology in 1904 to the merger of Lancashire with Yorkshire college in 1958, an average of only one student per annum (fifty-four out of a total of 265) achieved Manchester's BD, four on the basis of a BSc rather than a BA—no bad thing.[47] Within the same time span, twenty gained the MA by research, of whom six did not hold the BD.[48]

From the ranks of those who have had the most extensive education have normally been drawn the theological "resource persons" of the church, including its college principals, lecturers and professors. When, in 1850, W. Hendry Stowell addressed his students on becoming president of Cheshunt College, he said, "It will be increasingly easy, in all coming time, to find scholars. I pray that it may be not less easy to find men of original power . . . to preach the Gospel."[49] Others may determine how we are currently placed regarding ministers of original power who can preach the gospel; my point is that with hindsight we can see that Stowell was over-optimistic regarding scholars. As long ago as 1937, at a time of relative glut as compared with our situation today—even allowing for the diminution in the church's membership since he spoke—A. J. Grieve could lament, "I

---

46. In the middle decades of the twentieth century Yorkshire United College was a veritable nest of provincial moderators: John Buckingham, W. J. Coggan, J. A. Figures, W. Andrew James, and H. S. Stanley.

47. In the same period twenty-eight out of 167 (the figures are approximate) Yorkshire United College students completed both degrees.

48. Though four, who had been students between 1904 and 1958 subsequently gained the MA, including J. H. Eric Hull, whose resulting, still cited, book, *The Holy Spirit in the Acts of the Apostles*, is indicative of the high standard expected by the examiner's of Manchester's research MA as originally constituted.

49. Stowell, *An Address to the Students of Cheshunt College*, 12.

could wish that we had more *scholars* amongst us today."[50] We need to nurture those we have, and continually to seek out and support young men and women of academic promise. It should not be as difficult as it is to provide competent staff for our remaining colleges, expert participants in theological and ecumenical discussion, and those who can in local and regional contexts train and encourage elders and others in their several ministries. I specified the need of "young" men and women of academic promise (a) because if we expect our scholars both to undertake research in their fields and to have good pastoral experience, many will be forty before they are fully prepared; and (b) because I strongly dispute the attitude, rightly denounced by Figures, that people should not enter the ministry until they have had "experience of life." Somebody once told me in all seriousness that "You cannot be a minister if you have not driven a bus for twenty years." It may be that we have some ministers who were very good bus drivers. More worryingly, some who should know better have said more or less the same thing: "Ideally every pastor should first gain experience in the secular world," pronounced an authority on theological education.[51] Although Kinsler wrote this forty years ago, the sentiment lingers in some quarters. The fact is that no minister can possibly have experienced everything likely to befall the saints. We have to beware of the slippery slope at the bottom of which lies the claim "You cannot be a prison chaplain if you have not been a convict." More serious, however, is the dubious theology which lies behind the recommendation to delay the enrolment of the young on principle. For the call to ministry is of God, and while the call must rigorously be tested, the time of its arrival cannot be determined by us. Nothing that I have written is intended to disparage those who are ordained later in life, either as full-time ministers or as non-stipendiary ones.

Fourthly, we must ask whether at the present time we are doing enough with the candidates we have to draw out their scholarly gifts. To put it bluntly: if, as I believe and as many agree, one size does not fit all where ministerial education is concerned, have we cheated some if, in circles where internship training prevails (which no doubt ideally meets the needs of some),[52] the programme is not modified (as it can be and has

50. Grieve, "Christian Learning and Christian Living," 78.

51. Kinsler, in a duplicated paper on "Bases for Change in Theological Education," 1977, 10.

52. This form of training was introduced at Northern College with the arrival in 1979 of Principal R. J. McKelvey. He had pioneered such training in South Africa, see his paper, "Internship Training for Minister in South Africa."

been in some institutions) in such a way as to meet the needs of students who need to keep their noses in books for six years? Have we enabled them to make the most of the gifts they have been given? It is a theological as well as an educational question. I was appalled when a student came to see a seminary president with whom I was in conversation, in order to make an appointment to discuss with him the possibility that she might proceed to the PhD. At once he replied, "Why do you want to do that? You're only going to be a parish minister." She departed, downcast. He then said to me, "She's the brightest student in her year." Now (a) we do not have so many really able students in our pastoral ministries that we can afford not to encourage those who have the gifts to pursue their scholarly dream; and (b) the president's attitude seemed to be an irrational, even a cruel, refusal to encourage the development of a competent person's God-given gift.

I have stated that a minority of students only followed the courses I did, but I wish to make it clear, against any who may be inclined to question the point, that it was possible to gain a wide range of experience without detriment to rigorous academic, and supplementary college, courses. Certainly I never felt deprived of pastoral contact with real people and churches during those years of study. As I have said, almost every Sunday students were preaching far and wide and receiving hospitality from people of all types. I found myself among coal miners (and went down a mine) in the East Lancashire coalfield; among farmers in Cheshire villages; I staggered around Pendle Hill in my Sunday best between services at Colne; I became acquainted with life in suburban Liverpool and downtown Manchester, and with the lifestyles of industrial magnates in Yorkshire. During one summer vacation I worked for a high-class grocer in Surrey, who required his minions to weigh and pack almost uncontrollable coffee beans in folded and elegantly tucked-in sheets of paper (bags were taboo); and in two other vacations I toiled on a fruit farm, thinning apples and dodging wasps, and conducting worship in Surrey towns and villages on most Sundays. I had two consecutive three-month-long summer pastorates at the same northern church, and preached there once per month during the intervening academic year. Whilst there I conducted my first funeral service—in fact it was the first funeral I have ever attended ("You're not from up here, are you?" enquired the undertaker as we walked in front of the coffin to the Sunday School building: "You'll enjoy it! We see 'em off well up here! None of your china tea cups and fancy cakes—you'll get a good ham tea!"). I had never known a church with its own recreation ground with two tennis courts, a cricket pitch and a league-playing cricket team; with vast Scout and Guide activity; with a Rose Queen Festival; Whit Walks; and an annual sell-out pantomime over six days every winter. We worshipped in the Sunday School building because the church was suffering from mining subsidence, and I found myself at meetings with the local Member of Parliament and representatives of the Coal Board; and we conducted a house-to-house visitation campaign. All of this was most formative, not a little exhausting, and invaluable. I round off this point by referring to Kenneth Wadsworth's account of his visit to Open Day at Northern College in 1990. Having referred to the pattern of internship training then in operation he concluded,

> The inquiring visitor . . . may have asked about the provision of opportunity for retreat and quiet contemplation (as well as reflection on practical work), care for the maintenance of high standards of theological study and academic disciplines, and for the provision of teachers and thinkers for the next generation of ministerial training and Christian apologetic in a sceptical world. No doubt governors and staff have such concerns (as well as flexibility, relevance and communication) clearly in mind.[53]

Kenneth Wadsworth was a wise (Yorkshire College) man, who believed in holding together what needs to be held together.

Fifthly, secular university degree or certificate courses do not, by themselves, suffice to equip students for the ministry of the gospel, for the supply of Christian ministers is not directly among the objectives of the institutions which award them. While the intellectual rigour they provide is of real benefit to ministerial students, the university theological courses (like all other courses) must be open to all, including those of other faiths, and atheists, humanists, and those who have the wit see that a degree in theology can "deliver" a number of useful "transferable skills"—literary, philosophical, linguistic, historical, cross-cultural among them. Such universities must not assume, still less require, religious commitment on the part of their students. Moreover, the faculty of theology classroom in a secular university is not a mission hall; it should be a place of lively debate, not of dogmatic utterance—least of all if the regurgitation of dogma favoured by the lecturer is the condition of obtaining of good marks. It is well if intending ministers are within earshot of such debates—and it is even better if they are willing and constructive participants in them; but this is not, and never was, all they need. Such courses were always supplemented

53. Wadsworth, "Open to the World," 12.

by others conducted by the colleges. In more recent times ministers have been educated, often on a part-time basis, in regional centres, and in other lands as well.

In view of the diverse types of training received by candidates for ordination, and with reference to the fourfold ministerial task of conducting worship, preaching the gospel, and caring for and educating the flock, the question arises whether the church, which takes seriously its responsibility of interviewing those who offer themselves for the ministry before their courses begin, ought not to be equally concerned to examine them during their final year of training, and before they accept a call to service? Such a searching, oral, examination would be directly related to the fourfold ministerial task. It would be designed to ensure that the candidates for ordination have a lively grasp of the Bible; that they are knowledgeable as to the heritage of The United Reformed Church; that they understand the history and principles of Reformed worship; that they are conversant with the nature, objectives and styles of preaching; and that they understand the fundamental principles of pastoral care and Christian education. I also think that they should deliver a sermon in a church in the presence of an expert in voice production, so as to ascertain whether or not their vocal function is healthy. This has too often been the Cinderella of ministerial education (and it is not the same as elocution), yet the voice is the minister's instrument, and it needs to be thoroughly understood and efficiently used. If candidates are found wanting in any of the specified areas, help should be given before they are ordained.

A required two-year probationary and stipendiary course would be even better, if the ways and means could be found to mount it. Probationers could be inducted to a pastorate and ordained on successful completion of the course. The course might be conducted *via* a variety of methods, though I should hope that the probationers would come together from time to time for classes and fellowship. I should also hope that assessment would be rigorous, and that detailed knowledge and thoughtful presentations, both written and oral, would be expected. The course would include (a) liturgical studies, with special reference to the worship of the Reformed tradition(s); (b) homiletics, including the history of preaching with analysis of selected sermons through the centuries with regard to the context in which they were delivered, the exegesis presented and the objectives sought; the principles and practice of preaching (including the almost lost art of dividing a text); and (very importantly and too frequently incompetently handled) voice production and presentation in general (since, as every actor knows, even "getting on and getting off" are important, and in the context of worship such things make a theological statement; (c) pastoral theology with careful theological analysis of the doctrines of humanity, often tacitly held, which underlie secular models of counselling, and with reference to the situation in which the probationer is placed; (d) Christian education, with reference to the psychology of human development, and with particular reference to the history, principles and order of The United Reformed Church and its predecessors: this with a view to facilitating church practice, the training of confirmation/membership candidates, and participation in ecumenical discussions. In addition, I should like all probationers to sit four examinations (with context questions) covering the whole of the English Bible.

Whether gained (as far as possible) through an oral examination during a candidate's last year of training, or through a successfully completed probationary course, the church would have some confidence that whether persons had been trained largely through university courses, or internship, integrated or part-time courses, all of its ministers had had their disciplinary knowledge orientated towards the work of the ministry; that they would know their Bibles, and not simply certain set texts; and that they had the means of meeting the needs of the saints in respect of worship, preaching, pastoral care, and Christian education. With such competent ministers of the gospel, would not the confidence of all the other minister-saints increase as they became ever more secure in the faith and eager to love God with heart, mind and strength? Would not the church's mission be re-invigorated?

The objective of theological education for the ministry of the gospel is the formation of those who as well as being people of prayer and sincerity, are people imbued with godly learning. Let us have no false distinction between "formation" and "information," for spirituality is not innocent of doctrine, and theological study is formative. Ministers are people who have been made by the gospel—"trophies of grace," to use the old term—and who have made the gospel their own: "The ministry will soon wear out 'reach-me-down' convictions and reveal them in all their threadbare shabbiness," predicted John Huxtable.[54]

Dedicated and competent under-shepherds of the good Shepherd will be apt to lead the flock in praise, feed it with the Word, serve it with loving pastoral care, and teach its members the faith. All of which may seem so

---

54. Huxtable, "Thoughts on Ministerial Training," 143.

much old hat. In fact nothing could be more radical, for genuine ministry flows from the root (*radix*) who is Christ the Vine, in whom all his people are one. His is the primary ministry. God the Father calls his Son's co-workers, and they—ministers of the gospel and all the saints in their diverse ministries—witness to the gospel of saving grace by word and deed within and beyond the church. They do not, and could not, do this in their own strength. Rather, the power comes from the life-giving Holy Spirit (2 Cor 3:6). To repeat: in the deepest sense, the context of all Christian ministry is the saving activity, gracious call and divine commission of God the holy Trinity.

> My gracious Lord, I own thy right
> To every service I can pay;
> And call it my supreme delight
> To hear thy dictates and obey.
> Philip Doddridge (1702–51)

# Appendix 1

## The Trinitarian Blessing[1]

I TAKE AS MY "text" the following paragraph from the Revd Nick Stanyon's reflections on The United Reformed Church's recently published worship material: "Efforts to move away from traditional language in Trinitarian formulae have pitfalls. Liturgies may not necessarily be Trinitarian, just because they are in three parts. And there is a danger of slipping into modalism when we replace one 'name' of the Trinity with a job description, i.e. 'creator.'"[2]

Behind this cautionary word there lies a widespread and sometimes explosive debate. It is a debate in which my work has from time to time involved me, in academic and church contexts in a variety of cultures around the world. So sensitive is the issue that those seeking to tackle it need to make their position very clear lest they be misunderstood.

For example, Christians like myself who are committed to using the orthodox language of Father, Son, and Holy Spirit are dismissed by some as being "anti-women" because we confess that God is our "Father." Nothing could be further from the truth in my case. Like the apostle Paul, I do not wish to boast, but I think that I have done as much as any to raise the question of the place of women, not least of women in the ministry of the gospel, in a number of Reformed churches around the world in which to

---

1. This is a revised and slightly expanded version of an article published in *Reform* (May 2004) 20–21. At various points I have drawn material from my book, *Enlightenment, Ecumenism, Evangel*, 365–75.

2. Stanyon, Letter, 25.

date women are absent from that ministry. This is the gist of my case: If the sovereign God of all grace and mercy calls our one people by his Spirit through the Word; and if in that called community the barriers are broken down between male and female, bond and free (Gals 3:28; Col 3:11); and if God should then determine to call this woman or this man to be his ministers, on what conceivable grounds may we deny his right so to do? This is one of the cases where, as it seems to be, the churches at large are gradually catching up with the gospel—albeit at a depressingly slow place in some cases.

Another instance of catching up concerns inclusive language. Some years ago I came to the conclusion that in my writing and speaking it is consistent with the gospel that I do not use language which excludes half the human race. So when referring to males and females together, I use language which clearly embraces both. At the same time, I draw the line at damning all earlier writers as "sexist." They were not: they were simply working within the conventions of their time. In every generation there are things which, from the point of view of later generations, those living in it did not "see." Accordingly, a little humility will incline us to wonder in which connections people two hundred years hence will be tempted to regard us as having been benighted.

The really big question, however, concerns the language appropriately to be used of the Godhead. There are those who do not believe that masculine personal pronouns should be used of God, because this suggests that God is male, a man. But then sometimes the same people say that because the Greek word for "wisdom" is feminine, it refers to the feminine side of God. What it actually betokens is a convention of the Greek language. The Greek work for "sin" is a feminine noun, but nobody expects us to infer that sin originates in our "feminine" side. The moral is that we are on treacherous ground if we attempt to argue from the grammatical conventions of particular languages to substantive theological claims.

What is the positive case for retaining masculine personal pronouns when the reference is to God? My answer is that I use such pronouns because I believe it extremely important that Christians use language which makes it abundantly clear that the Godhead is personal. To do this I need personal pronouns. Pronouns may be masculine, feminine, or neuter. I cannot bring myself to use the neuter pronoun and refer to God as "it." If I were to begin to use feminine pronouns in the interests of balance, somebody somewhere might think that I have now decided that God is a woman—which I have not, since God is neither male nor female and it is idolatrous to think otherwise: God is spirit. To avoid pronouns altogether by repeating "God" ("God sent God's Son into God's world to save God's people from their sins") makes for stylistic awkwardness, not to mention boredom. More importantly, it fails to make explicit God's personal nature: "God" might, for example, refer to that "certain Something" in which many people profess to believe when confronted by pollsters. Because God is neither a man nor a woman, conventions regarding the use of language in the human context cannot (logically) apply to him.

More serious still is the debate surrounding the threefold name: Father, Son, and Holy Spirit. It would be quite wrong to suppose that all feminists oppose this formula. But some feminists, distressed by what they see as biblical and ecclesiastical patriarchalism, do not use, and do not wish others to hear, the threefold Name because of its reference to God as Father. Others say, "I cannot call God 'Father' because my own father was a bullying tyrant." That anyone should have had such a human father is deeply sad. But we cannot elevate such particular unfortunate experiences into the lens through which we view the whole of Christian doctrine. It might even be suggested that God's holy, loving fatherhood is precisely what reveals the gulf between it and even the noblest expression of human fatherhood.

It goes without saying that there are many other blessings which may be used in worship, but I do not think that we have adequate grounds for quietly shelving the blessing in the name of Father, Son and Holy Spirit. There are both theological and ethical (not to mention ecumenical) issues at stake here.

Theologically, when people substitute terms like "Creator, Redeemer, and Sustainer" for the three persons they are using functional terms which do not make it clear that the Godhead is personal—these are what Mr. Stanyon calls items in God's "job description." More importantly, this practice loses the inner-personal relations of the Godhead, and obscures the important point that the Godhead is intimately involved in the actions of all the persons. If this idea is lost then, as Mr. Stanyon suggests, modalism—even tritheism (the doctrine that there are three gods)—threatens. It is the one triune God—Father, Son, and Holy Spirit—who (not "which") is Creator, Redeemer, Sustainer, and much else besides.

Underlying this debate is the distinction between metaphor and analogy. If a psalmist says that God is a rock or a fortress we are in the realm of metaphor, for God is not literally either of these. Many metaphors are used of God in the Bible, and some are feminine. We should do well to use a wider range of these than we do in our worship and devotions. But in the trinitarian formula "Father" is an analogy, and analogies can be both positive and negative. There is a claimed basis of identity, a "likeness," between the Father of all and human fatherhood (in a way that there is not between God and a rock), but there are profound differences too: human fathers are male, God is not, and so on.

But why, it might be asked, may we not construct an analogy using "Mother"? Here we come finally to the authority of Scripture and to the experience of Christians. There can be no question that Jesus called God "Father," and taught us to do the same; but, as a Jew, he would never have fallen for the idolatry of thinking that God was a man. The experience of the early Christians was that through Jesus Christ they had found new life and forgiveness of sins—but who can save but God? They experienced reinvigoration following despair, and courageously set forth on a mission against great odds—but who can so motivate a church but the Spirit of God? Clearly, the doctrine of the Trinity was not the finding of a committee. Rather, on the basis of the biblical clues, it is an account of what God had made known and the early Christians had experienced. The early Christians did not ask themselves what images would be most appropriately used of God. They spoke of God as he had shown himself to be in their experience; and as he has shown himself to be, so he is—otherwise there has not been a revelation of God.

If this is so, the ethical question arises when some who lead our worship habitually exclude the Trinitarian blessing. Those who lead worship do not do so as private persons, choosing their favourite biblical passages and hymns, and making their personal prayers. They are public persons with the privilege of leading the worship of the people—and the people are a trinitarian people. The first sentence of "The Faith of the United Reformed Church" in our Basis of Union crisply situates us in the catholic faith of the ages and invokes the threefold name: "The United Reformed Church confesses the faith of the Church Catholic in one God, Father, Son and Holy Spirit."[3] It is also affirmed that the Church has a "duty to be open at all times to the leading of the Holy Spirit and therefore affirms its right to make such new declarations of its faith and for such purposes as from time to time may be required in obedience to the same Spirit."[4]

3. Bush, *The Manual*, 12.
4. Ibid., 14.

I believe that unless or until it becomes "commonly agreed among us" that we ought no longer to use the threefold name in worship (which conclusion would, for good or ill, place us outside the mainstream of historic Christianity), those who lead our worship are morally obliged to retain and use the Trinitarian formula along with other blessings. If their personal conscientious conviction will not permit this, they ought first to seek to change the mind of the Church. If this fails they may need to consider their position. Not a few have done this over the centuries. For example, Thomas Belsham, one of my predecessors at Angel Street, Worcester, became a tutor at the Dissenting academy at Daventry in 1781. Whilst there he embraced Unitarian views, resigned his post in 1789, and removed to the academy which the Rational Dissenters established at Hackney. I believe that his action both exemplifies personal integrity, and also implies his realization that those committed to a trinitarian framework for their Christian life and worship, which he could no longer endorse, ought not to be denied it.

I am not pleading for heresy trials. Rather, I am seeking to recognise the need to honour the consciences of both worship leaders and the Church, and to uphold the integrity of both. Only if an amicable solution in a particular case could not be reached, and if pastoral relations broke down, would the question of church discipline hove into view.

I have attempted to set down in orderly yet brief fashion matters which drive to the heart of our faith, and upon which the nature of our worship and our ecumenical relations turn. I very much hope that these matters will receive due and gracious attention as The United Reformed Church reviews its life and witness.

# Appendix 2

## The Councils of The United Reformed Church

AT THE TIME OF the union in 1972 of the Presbyterian Church of England with the Congregational Church in England and Wales to form The United Reformed Church, four councils were established:

a. The Church Meeting and the Elder's Meeting of each local church.

b. The Council of each District to be known as a District Council.

c. The Synod of each province to be known as a Provincial Synod.

d. The General Assembly of the United Reformed Church.

According to the Scheme of Union, all of these are to understand themselves as being under the authority of God's Word and the Holy Spirit:

> These four parts of the Structure of the United Reformed Church shall have such consultative, legislative and executive functions as are hereinafter respectively assigned to each of them and each shall be recognised by members of the United Reformed Church as possessing such authority, under the Word of God and the promised guidance of the Holy Spirit, as shall enable it to exercise its functions and thereby to minister in that sphere of the life of the United Reformed Church with which it is concerned.[1]

What this means in a nutshell is that in the United Reformed Church we seek to discern the mind of Christ, the only Head of the church, by the

1. Bush, ed., *The Manual*, 21.

Spirit, through the Word, within the fellowship (always remembering that local fellowships belong to wider ones, and that they inherit the testimony of the church of past ages). If the Spirit alone is emphasized you can end up with the spirit of the most powerful individuals, or of the age; if the Word alone is emphasized you can be at the mercy of those who uncritically insist that "It's in the Book!" If you think only of the immediate fellowship you can land in granular independency. But when these three are in harmony then you have such necessary checks and balances as will permit the confidence that the objective of discerning the mind of Christ is not altogether unachievable. Nothing constitutes a graver threat to our practice than the voting system which still prevails in some quarters. What needs to be discovered through prayer and testimony, is what the Quakers call "the sense of the meeting."

I mention in passing the facts that, to the regret of many, District Councils have subsequently been abolished, and that on financial grounds General Assemblies are nowadays held once every two years only. A representative Mission Council serves as the General Assembly's executive body, and has the responsibility of ensuring that whatever is done in the name of the Church serves the overall mission of the Church.

Since I have already discussed the Church Meeting in chapter 3, I am left with two councils to mention, of which the first is the Synod. No less than the Church Meeting, the Synod is charged with seeking the will of Christ in respect of its range of responsibilities. The office of Synod Moderator, originally primarily concerned with the pastoral care of ministers and churches, has in recent time, and in some cases, transmogrified into a more executive position: this to the dismay of some. The office is currently under review.[2] The Moderator conducts the meetings of Synod, and these are concerned with the mission to the region, church extension, ecumenical relations, Christian education, and the making of recommendations both to local churches and to the General Assembly.

The General Assembly, "shall embody the unity of the United Reformed Church and act as the central organ of its life and the final authority, under the Word of God and the promised guidance of the Holy Spirit, in all matters of doctrine and order, and in all other concerns of its life."[3] It is a representative assembly, charged "to oversee the total work of the Church."[4]

2. See further D. R. Peel's stimulating study, *The Story of the Moderators*.

3. Ibid., 27.

4. Ibid, 27.

I now come to the crucial doctrinal point in all of this. The underlying principle of the polity of The United Reformed Church is that of mutual episcope. Ours is precisely not a church with an hierarchy of church courts. The *Scheme of Union* consistently refers to nearer and farther church councils—the term "court" nowhere appears. The conviction is that, under the guidance of the Holy Spirit, the mind of Christ, the one Head of the church, is capable of being sought and found at all three *foci* (I do not say "levels") of churchly life. The question thus arises, what happens if, for example, on a particular issue a Church Meeting reaches one decision and the General Assembly another? The answer is that the General Assembly's initial ruling does not necessarily prevail, and it has not always done so. That is to say, there is provision for appeal, for mutual consultation, and for the rescinding of an Assembly decision. This is in accordance with a very important affirmation that "Decisions on the part of any Council shall be reached only after the fullest attempt has been made to discover the mind of the other Councils or of local churches likely to be affected by the decision."[5] Had the emphasis upon the mutuality of oversight as between the several *foci* not been made, it is quite possible that the union would not have come about.

Tony Tucker has rightly said that "The new Church which emerged in 1972 was neither a resurrected Congregational Church in England and Wales nor a resurrected Presbyterian Church of England. It was evident that both these churches had laid down their separate existences, and that the United Reformed Church was not a continuation of either of its predecessors under a new name."[6] Three pages later he declares that "The new Church—united and reformed—was therefore to be recognisably 'presbyterian' in its structure."[7] This is not helpful, because the inverted commas around "presbyterian" might be taken as suggesting that the structure of The United Reformed Church is "presbyterian-like," or "Presbyterian in all but name," when in significant respects it is neither. For example, many of the Presbyterians had been brought up with Scottish roots in, or memories of, an hierarchy of church courts (something which some early English Presbyterians, peering over the Scottish border, branded an "exotic novelty"). The distinguished Presbyterian P. Carnegie Simpson, writing on "The Character of Presbytery" in a Congregational journal, explained,

5. Ibid., 29.

6. Tucker, *Reformed* Ministry, 98. See also Sell, *Saints: Visible, Orderly and Catholic*, 116–20.

7. Tucker, *Reformed Ministry*, 101.

with italics, that "We have what may be described as a *hierarchy of church courts*. The session has authority over a congregation; the presbytery over a district; the synod or assembly over the whole church." He adds that "there is a well-defined right of appeal from the decision of a lower court to a higher."[8] The implication, however, is that no appeal against the finding of the highest court is possible, while the church membership as a totality in any given congregation is not regarded as a deliberative council. The notion of hierarchy and courts, and the repeated phrase "authority over" combine to suggest that we are not in the realm of nearer and farther councils all, in an atmosphere of mutual episcope, seeking the guidance of the Holy Spirit and the mind of Christ. But this *is* the operative principle in The United Reformed Church, and clearly Church Meeting is a council of the Church. Former Presbyterians could not deny that God the Holy Spirit may address the saints in Church Meeting; former Congregationalists could not deny that the same Spirit may inform the decisions of wider (not higher) councils—a conclusion they had already reached when, in 1966, they ceased to be The Congregational Union of England and Wales and became The Congregational Church in England and Wales.[9]

Concern over this issue was among the most significant factors which prompted some, in the interests of their understanding of the autonomy of the local church, not to go forward with the Congregational Church. Others who had been troubled over the issue were able to proceed once the assurance was given that mutual oversight would prevail, and this principle was carried forward into The United Reformed Church. Theologically and logically it could not be otherwise. Once the theological judgment is made that each council of the Church is competent to seek and discern the mind of Christ under the guidance of the Holy Spirit, there cannot be an hierarchy of "church courts" (it is a logical "cannot"), because although the several councils have their specific terms of reference, their concerns and interests will quite frequently overlap. Hence, in a case of disagreement between a local church's decision and that of the General Assembly, for example, and on the assumption that both parties have examined the issue with integrity and that neither was being deliberately wilful; and on the

8. Simpson, "The Character of Presbytery," 310.

9. For which saga see Sell, *Testimony and Tradition*, ch. 12. On the particular point see Sell, *Saints: Visible, Orderly and Catholic*, 113–14. On the latter page the following pamphlet is quoted: *Oversight and Covenant. Interim Report of Commission No. 1. Some Questions and Answers*, London: Congregational Union of England and Wales, n.d., Q and A 6.

further, fundamental, assumption that the Holy Spirit does not speak with a forked tongue and say one thing to one party and something different to another on the same issue, elementary logic suggests that while one party or the other may be in the right, or both may be mistaken, they cannot both be right. Such disagreement is by no means necessarily wilful: a Church Meeting may, for example, lack required expertise in a given area, or the General Assembly may lack relevant local knowledge, and either or both of these may explain the absence of shared discernment. The remedy lies in further mutual consultation in an atmosphere of trust and prayer, with any parting of the ways being the last resort.

Again, whereas the Presbyterians had regarded the presbytery (comprising a number of congregations) as the local church (which is why the totality of members in a particular place was not deemed to be a "court"), the Congregationalists always thought of the local church as the covenanted saints and children of the covenant within particular congregations, albeit (when they remembered it) these as being outcrops of the one church catholic. It was particularly gracious of the Presbyterians to adopt the idea of the regular Church Meeting, and also the ministry of regional moderators, things that they had never previously experienced. These decisions were not made in a spirit of give and take, still less of "ecclesiastical horse-trading," but following study of the doctrinal principles concerning the sole Lordship of Christ and the guidance of the Holy Spirit that I have outlined. The upshot is that anyone who says that at the union the Congregationalists allowed themselves to fall for the Presbyterian order, or that the Presbyterians put their heads into the noose of granular independency, is speaking far less than the truth.

As with Church Meeting, so with the other councils: they comprise saints who are also sinners. Thus, for example, at General Assembly there can be ungodly politicking, the packing of meetings, and an over-enthusiasm on the part of deeply committed people, which can verge upon the untruthful. There was an example of this when it was loudly proclaimed that with the founding of The United Reformed Church in 1972, two Christian traditions which had stood apart for three hundred years had come together in the first transconfessional union this country had seen. This was really stretching things a little. In fact, most of the Presbyterians of Old Dissent had become Congregationalists by the end of the eighteenth century, while a significant number of them had become Unitarians. With whom, then, did the English and English-speaking Welsh Congregationalists unite?

With the Presbyterian Church of England of 1876. This Church resulted from the union of the Presbyterian Church *in* England, which comprised almost all of the Church of Scotland's churches on English soil (and which stood with the Free Church of Scotland at the Disruption of 1843) with the churches of the United Presbyterian Church of Scotland which had been planted in England, both of which denominations had absorbed remnant trinitarian Presbyterian churches of Old Dissent.

Recalling my assertion that in The United Reformed Church we seek to discern the mind of Christ by the Spirit, through the Word, within the fellowship, I conclude by affirming that the fellowship, though at one and the same time visible, local, and catholic, also comprises the saints of yesteryear, whose witness flows down to us through writings, monuments, and memories. It behoves us to know our heritage, in order that we may benefit from the insights of our forebears, conduct ourselves with integrity, and have something to bring to the ecumenical table; but we should not restrict our attention to it. We are never more true to our non-sectarian, catholic, principle than when we sing,

> The saints on earth and those above
> But one communion make;
> Join'd to their Lord in bonds of love,
> All of his grace partake.
> (Charles Wesley, 1707–88)

# Appendix 3

## A Charge to the Minister and the Church[1]

**READINGS: PROVERBS 3:1–12; HEBREWS 12:1–13; MATTHEW 11:25–30.**

I speak to you in the name of God, Father, Son, and Holy Spirit.

### TEXT: "THE LORD DISCIPLINES THOSE WHOM HE LOVES" (HEBREWS 12:6)

Now isn't that just like a minister of religion? Here we are, on a pleasant sunny day. We have survived a pastoral vacancy during which we worked our socks off (and some of us are now hoping for a bit of a rest). We have called our next minister, and we are looking forward to exciting times ahead, not to mention the tea following this service. And he wants to talk about the gloomy subject of discipline!

Well I do; because when writers use a word eight times in six verses they are making a great effort to get something over to us. And that is

---

1. I have habitually declined requests to publish my sermons because sermons are performed events prepared for particular people in particular circumstances. Left on the page, sermons are flat, even though, as in this case, they may be written in spoken English. This is because the context is removed, the variations in pitch, tone, and volume cannot be heard, the twinkling of the eye cannot be seen, and the pauses cannot be registered. For the first and only time I break my rule because this sermon summarizes much of what I have attempted to say in this book.

how the writer to the Hebrews (whoever he was) uses this word "discipline." To him "discipline" is a very important word, though he knows that what it stands for is not a very popular thing: "Discipline, to be sure, is never pleasant," he says. This is because he is thinking especially of the trials which befall God's people. Those to whom he was writing had not yet "resisted to the point of shedding blood," but possible persecution was just around the corner. Nevertheless, following the book of Proverbs, from which he quotes, he insists that discipline is the badge of sonship and daughterhood: "The Lord disciplines those whom he loves." There is nothing spiteful or vindictive about the Father's discipline, though there is much about it that is testing and searching. To be loved by God, to be a son or daughter of God is to be disciplined by the heavenly Father. But, he solemnly continues, "If you escape the discipline in which all sons [and daughters] share, you must be illegitimate and not true sons [or daughters]." The Authorised Version of the Bible makes him say that those who escape the Father's discipline are bastards. Well, you know where you are with a writer like that! He pulls no punches.

Now what has all of this to do with what we are doing today? Before I've done I shall talk about the trials which can befall the people of God today. But first I'm going to break a rule of sermon-making and throw the net more widely than the writer to the Hebrews does in this passage. I wish to remind minister and people that you stand under the discipline of the Word; under the discipline of the church; and under the discipline of circumstances. So, you see, I'm breaking a rule, but you will still have three points!

First, then, you stand under the discipline of the Word. It is a gospel word—a good news word. By the grace of God, "We have heard the joyful sound, Jesus saves!" This is the word to be proclaimed. This is the word to be received. While you may go among folk in genial humanist fashion, you will not engage in effective outreach for Christ's sake unless you have been gripped by this word.

It is the special responsibility of ministers of the gospel to preach this Word. It should be their greatest delight, as it is their greatest privilege, to do so. To be able to tell men and women, boys and girls of the overflowing love of God towards the undeserving; to be able to direct them to the Cross, where, in Christ, God acts victoriously for the redemption of his world is a task as challenging as it is urgent. Why, then, do I hear some Christians saying that the day of preaching is over? "People cannot listen for long;

they can only digest sound bites." How utterly patronising! They can concentrate on a football commentary from beginning to end. In any case, the
tidings of the gospel are so grand, and its warnings so solemn, that they
had better listen to it. Or again, "Ministers feel that they are just preaching
to the converted all the time." But if they were, would not the converted be
reaching out to those who are not, and then the ministers wouldn't be doing that. For those who have really been engrafted into Christ as branches
of the Vine, cannot but testify to what they have seen and heard. Even
ministers are sometimes tempted to question the place of preaching, and
sometimes make desperate efforts to replace it, rather than supplement it,
with dramatic interludes or religious dance. "We don't want to be six feet
above criticism," they declare; as if in preaching they are simply trotting out
their latest thoughts on this and that. Well, if that is what they are doing,
their silence is preferable. For the minister's task is an ambassadorial one;
and ambassadors gets their message from the king; they do not concoct
it, or otherwise scratch around for it—even on Google. Ministers are the
announcers of God's good tidings, the edifiers of God's flock; and I say that
we need more of that, not less. And we need it to be based on the most
thorough homework of which we are capable, and to grow out of our most
ardent prayer. It is true that ministers are not responsible for the results of
their preaching (something that church members need to remember when
the pews don't suddenly fill up). It is true, as my friend Thomas Watson,
who died in 1686 said, "The ministers of God are only the pipes and organs; it is the Spirit blowing in them, that effectually changes the heart."
But ministers are responsible for their consecrated effort—or lack of it. I
am not pleading for great oratory, or pulpit fireworks: just for honest toil;
for workers who have no need to be ashamed of their efforts to preach the
gospel of which none need be ashamed. It still pleases God to save people
through the hearing of the word. Then let us proclaim that word. And if, in
genuine humility we say to God, like Jeremiah of old, "I cannot speak for I
am a child" (in Lancashire parlance he meant, "no'but a lad"), back comes
God's reply, "I have put my words in your mouth." Hear then the stately
words of the Westminster Larger Catechism, prepared in the seventeenth
century by our Presbyterian and Congregational forebears:

> They that are called to labour in the ministry of the word, are to
> preach sound doctrine, diligently, in season and out of season;
> plainly, not in the enticing words of man's wisdom, but in demon-
> stration of the Spirit, and of power; faithfully, making known the

whole counsel of God; wisely, applying themselves to the necessities and capacities of the hearers; zealously, with fervent love to God and the souls of the people; sincerely, aiming at his glory, and their conversion, edification, and salvation.

That remains a thorough and challenging statement of the preacher's objectives and manner.

Now, having tackled the minister, I feel free to turn upon the rest of you! For if the Word imposes a discipline upon those who preach, it also imposes a discipline upon those who hear. The next question in the Larger Catechism of 1648 is: "What is required of those that hear the word preached?" The answer is,

that they attend upon it with diligence, preparation, and prayer; examine what they hear by the scriptures; receive the truth with faith, love, meekness and readiness of mind, as the word of God; meditate and confer on it; hide it in their hearts, and bring forth the fruit of it in their lives.

You see, it is hard work really to hear a sermon. (You may be thinking it's certainly hard work to hear this one—but that's not what I mean.) The work begins before you arrive in church, as you prayerfully prepare yourself to hear the Word, and as you pray for the minister as he or she prepares to preach. The work continues after you leave the service, as you test what you hear against the scriptures, and as you are challenged to apply what you hear to yourself. Then you are to discuss it with other saints, retain the truth, and bring forth fruit compatible with it.

Be thirsty for the Word! Let you attitude be, "More about Jesus would I know." When the celebrated preacher, John Kennedy of Dingwall, was due to preach in the fishing district of Lochaber, one of the locals said to a fisherman member of the congregation, "What's the use of Dr. Kennedy going to preach to you folk in Lochaber? He will preach over your heads, and you'll make nothing of him." "I tell you," the old fisherman replied, "we have in Lochaber those that won't leave a bait on his hooks." Let that be your attitude. Be eager hearers of the Word. You are under its discipline no less than the minister.

Now the great thing God does through the gospel Word is to being the church into being. God, by the gospel, creates the church. Through the good news he calls out and gathers together his new people by the Holy Spirit. We do not make the church; we do not join the church. The church is a company into which we are engrafted by grace, so that we become limbs of the body, branches of Christ the Vine. To be united with him, to be of his company, is to be an adopted son or daughter; and to be adopted sons and daughters is to be disciplined. At the very heart of our corporate discipline is our accountability under God for our stewardship of the gospel we have received. We are a privileged people. We have received good news that we did not deserve. We are under the solemn responsibility of performing what should be a happy task—that of witnessing for Christ before others, by word and deed.

How often the people of God have tried to sidestep their mission! Let me update and paraphrase Amos for you. Uprooted from his sheep-farming duties by God's call, he comes before God's ancient people and begins to preach to them. In the name of God he says, "You only have I known of all the families of the earth . . ." and I imagine the hearers feeling rather pleased with themselves. "Yes," they think, "we are indeed God's people, in the line of Abraham, Isaac, and Jacob." A woman in the audience nudges her husband and whispers, "This Amos is a grand preacher: we must see if we can get him for the harvest festival." Her husband whispers back, "Good idea! And if we could get Amos to be our minister we'd even redecorate the crumbling manse." Then Amos finishes his sentence: "You only have I known . . . therefore I will punish you for all your iniquities." And they send him home without even covering the cost of his petrol!

The moral is that from those to whom much has been given, much will be expected. Where God is concerned, there is no privilege without responsibility. We need, therefore, with God's help, to equip ourselves to be the church; to tool ourselves up for mission. How do we know a true church when we see one? Many of the Reformed confessions and catechisms tell us, but nobody put it more succinctly than the converted Scottish Dominican, John Craig. In his 1581 catechism he declared that the marks of the church are, "The Word, the Sacraments, and discipline rightly exercised." It's that word "discipline" again. If you read our old hand-written church books (and if you know anyone who keeps some of these under their bed, do persuade them to pass them to those who can properly care for them): if you read these books you will see that our forebears in the faith regularly disciplined church members: for falling asleep during the sermon; for being drunk and disorderly; for keeping wicked men company, for malicious gossip. Sometimes, no doubt, they were clumsy. But at their best they knew, as John Owen and others told them, that "The nature and end of judgment must be corrective, not vindictive; for healing, not destruction." They knew that the objectives of church discipline were the honour of God, the integrity of the church, and the restoration of those who had fallen by the wayside. They knew what we sometimes forget, that if we become so identified with the culture around us, we forfeit our ability to speak a prophetic, counter-cultural, word to it. At their best they truly cared for one another and encouraged one another in the faith. We might say that the purpose of church discipline is to equip the church for its mission. We are entered corporately for a race, and we need to be in training. And where is the training camp for this mission? It is the Church Meeting. Here we seek not the majority will of the members of the church, but the will of the church's Lord. Church Meeting is a credal assembly, where we confess the Lordship of Christ the Head of the church—just as we did in Sunday worship, and we seek unanimity in him. Here we find out what he would have us to, and we seek his guidance as to the ways and means of taking the good news off our premises and into the world around.

Let us put away hindrances. Let us stick to the priorities. The diaries of some of our ministers are overweight. The programmes of some of our churches are so fat that the churches cannot move. We need to trim down. We need nourishing food and plenty of spiritual jogging. We need study and prayer and learning the faith even more than we need badminton and amateur dramatics. We need a balance; and when we have found it we will find that the members, making the objective of mission their own, really begin to pull together for the Lord's sake. When they do not, the results can be dire. Listen to this Russian fable: A pike, a crab, and a swan were given the task of pulling a truck up a hill. (Don't ask me why, this is a Russian fable.) They were all harnessed, they expended great effort, they nearly burst their skins, but all to no avail. It was not the load was difficult to move. But upward strained the swan towards the sky above; the crab kept stepping sideways; the pike made for the pond. And which was right and which was wrong, I neither know nor care. I only know the truck's still there.

I have spoken of the discipline of the Word and the discipline of the church. Now as we go forth in mission in the strength of God's grace, we shall find that time and we are disciplined us through circumstances. This, you remember, was the particular concern of the writer to the Hebrews; his readers needed to brace themselves against the possibility of harsh trials to come. Now when we think of being disciplined by circumstances, I suppose that our minds turn to the hard times and the rocky places. Ministers face these, and so do church members; and so do churches as corporate fellow-ships. There are times when nothing seems to go right; when we pipe and nobody dances; when we see little result for our efforts. It is then that we need to remember that the race for which we are entered is one to be run with perseverance. It is no quick sprint that we're in. We follow one who walked the hardest way of all. He is out before us as the pioneer, and he has not resigned. Upon him we depend; to him we look. He is the good Shepherd leading his flock, and he will even lay down his life for them. "The Lord disciplines those whom he loves," and he loves no one as he loves his Son; and Christ was not exempt from discipline. As Horatius Bonar invites us to sing,

> This is the way the Master went,
> Should not the servant tread it still?

Or, as Thomas Watson put it, "Was Christ crowned with thorns, and do we expect to be crowned with roses?"

However rough the way, we are, said Philip Doddridge, being brought to "better pastures . . . his hand will certainly conduct us to them; nor need we fear the darkest passage on the way." Charles Wesley agreed:

> By thine unerring Spirit led,
> We shall not in the desert stray . . .
> As fare from danger as from fear,
> While love, almighty love, is near.

As promised, I have spoken about the discipline of circumstances. That, after all, is what was uppermost in the mind of the writer to the He-brews. But there is one thing more: the discipline of success. A successful ministry can be dangerous. A successful church can be a dangerous place to be. Success can turn the head. As soon as ministers think that any success is solely due their toil or expertise, they need to take care. As soon as a church thinks that its flourishing state is all its own work, it needs to think again. The Christians at Laodicea thought they had it made. They were rich, they had everything they needed. They probably had a Senior Executive Pastor, half a dozen handbell choirs, and a bigger gymnasium than the Baptists down the road. But to the risen Christ they were "poor, blind and naked."

William Grimshaw of Haworth, that doughty Church of England evangelical of the eighteenth century, whose church grew by leaps and bounds under the preaching of the gospel, had the right idea. "When I die," he said, "I shall have my greatest grief and my greatest joy: my greatest grief that I have done so little for Jesus, and my greatest joy that Jesus has done so much for me. My last words shall be, Here goes an unprofitable servant." God uses and blesses people and churches like that: they give all the glory to him. As you run your race and minister and church, may no disciplining circumstances, sad, or happy, prevent you from doing likewise.

We, by God's grace, are his sons and daughters. God's sons and daughters are disciplined. We are under the kindly discipline of the Word, the church, and circumstances. Can we survive this discipline? I think we can, for as well as being our Shepherd, Jesus is an excellent carpenter. He makes a snugly fitting yoke, and to be yoked to him is life eternal. So, then, in the words of the letter to the Hebrews, "Come, then, stiffen your drooping arms and shaking knees, and keep your steps from wavering." In other words, get fit; set your bones; attend to dislocated knees, and run the race. Then you will be blessed; God will save others through your ministry; the cloud of witnesses will rejoice; and God shall have the glory. To his holy name be honour and praise now and for ever. Amen.

# Bibliography

## MANUSCRIPTS

*Abbreviation,* DWL = Dr. Williams's Library, London.

Baxter, Richard. MS 2.256, DWL.

Cocks, H. F. Lovell. "By Faith Alone," typescript, Lovell Cocks papers, DWL.

———. "Lectures on Preaching, II," Lovell Cocks papers, DWL.

Conder, John. "Divinity Lectures," transcribed by W. L. Bishop, New College, London MSS L28.1.2, DWL.

Kinsler, F. Ross. "Bases for Change in Theological Education," typescript in the author's possession.

Oman, John. "Memorandum" to the Moderator's committee on the ministry, Oman papers, Westminster College, Cambridge.

Western College Minute Book, The Congregational College Archives: Western College, Bristol, Box 45, the John Rylands University Library of Manchester.

## PUBLISHED WORKS

Achtemeier, P. Mark. "The *Union with Christ* doctrine in Renewal Movements of the Presbyterian Church (USA)." In *Reformed Theology: Identity and Ecumenicity,* edited by William M. Alston, Jr., and Michael Welker, 336–50, Grand Rapids: Eerdmans, 2003.

Anon. Advertisement in *Christianity Today,* 22 May 2000, 107.

———. *A Book of Services and Prayers.* London: Independent, 1959.

———. *Centenary of the Lancashire Independent College, 1816–1916, celebrated 1920.* Published by the College, 1920.

———. *The Directory for the Publick Worship of God,* 1645; bound with *The Westminster Confession of Faith.* Edinburgh: John Reid, 1689.

———. *Final Report* (Anglican/Roman Catholic International Commission). London: CTS/SPCK, 1982.

———. *A Manual for Ministers,* London: Independent, 1936.

———. *Minutes of the Proceedings of a Conference of Delegates from the Committees of Various Theological Colleges connected with the Independent Churches of England and Wales*. London: Blackburn and Pardon, 1845; and a second conference under the same title: London: Jackson, 1865.

———. *Oversight and Covenant. Interim Report of Commission No. I. Some Questions and Answers*. London: Congregational Union of England and Wales, n.d. (but 1960s).

———. *Patterns of Ministry in The United Reformed Church*, discussion paper, c. 1992.

———. "Rector and Doctor." *World Christian Digest* 50 (June 1953) 60.

———. *Rejoice and Sing*. Oxford: Oxford University Press, for The United Reformed Church, 1991.

———. *Report of the Senatus Academicus and Calendar of the Associated Colleges of England and Wales, 1885*. London: printed for the Senatus, 1885.

———. *Report of the Senatus Academicus of Associated Theological Colleges, British and Colonial, 1901*. London: printed for the Senatus, 1902.

———. *Service Book* [The United Reformed Church]. Oxford: Oxford University Press, 1989.

———. "Towards a Framework of a Theology and Practice of Ministry in the Presbyterian Church of Canada." Don Mills, ON: Board of Ministry, PCC, 1991.

Augustine. *On Christian Doctrine*. In *Select Library of Nicene and Post-Nicene Fathers*, Series I, II.iv. Edinburgh: T. & T. Clark, 1890.

Bacon, Francis. *Essays*, London: John Jaggard, 1613.

Barnes, Thomas. *A Discourse delivered at the Commencement of the Manchester Academy*. Warrington, UK: W. Eyres, 1786.

Barrie, J. M. *Auld Licht Idylls*. New York: Caldwell, n.d.

Baxter, Richard. *Autobiography*. (Abridged.) London: Dent, 1931.

———. *Gildas Salvianus: The Reformed Pastor*. London: Robert White for Nevil Simmons, 1657.

———. *Poetical Fragments*. London: T. Snowden for B. Simmons, 1681.

———. *Practical Works*. 23 vols. London: James Duncan, 1830.

Bender, Ross T. *Education for Peoplehood: Essays on the Teaching Ministry of the Church*. Elkhart, IN: Institute of Mennonite Studies, 1997.

Bennett, Arnold. *Anna of the Five Towns*. 1984. Reprint. Harmondsworth, UK: Penguin, 2002.

Bergler, Thomas E. "When Are We Going to Grow Up? The Juvenilization of American Christianity." *Christianity Today*, June 2003, 18–24.

Bonar, Andrew. *The Life of Robert Murray M'Cheyne*. 1844. Reprint. London: Banner of Truth, 1962.

Bourn, Samuel. *A Dialogue between a Baptist and a Churchman*. London: J. Roberts, 1737.

———. *The Young Christian's Prayer Book*. 4th ed. Birmingham: n.p., 1770.

Bradbury, Jen. "Sticky Faith." *The Christian Century*, 29 May 2013, 22–25.

Brentall, John M. *William Bagshawe, The Apostle of the Peak*. London: Banner of Truth, 1970.

Bridges, Charles. *The Christian Ministry with an Enquiry into the Causes of its Inefficiency*. 1830. Reprint. London: Banner of Truth, 1967.

Bunyan, John. *Grace Abounding to the Chief of Sinners*. 1666. Reprint. Harmondsworth, UK: Penguin, 1987.

Burder, Henry Forster. "The Objects and Progress of the Institution." In *An Address delivered on Laying the Foundation Stone of Highbury College, by the Rev. George*

*Clayton; and also Addresses delivered at the Opening of the College, by the Rev. H. F. Burder, M.A., and the Rev. W. Harris, LLD.* London: R. Clay, 1826.

Burrage, Champlin. *Early English Dissenters.* 2 vols. Cambridge: Cambridge University Press, 1912.

Bush, Percy W., ed. *The United Reformed Church . . . Manual.* London: The United Reformed Church, 1973.

Calvin, John. *Commentary on Ephesians.* Translated by T. H. L. Parker. Grand Rapids: Eerdmans, 1965.

————. *Institutes of the Christian Religion.* Translated by Ford Lewis Battles and edited by John T. McNeil. Philadelphia: Westminster, 1960.

Chandler. Samuel. *Preaching the Gospel a More Effectual Method of Salvation, than Human Wisdom and Philosophy. A Sermon preached at the Ordination of Mr. Thomas Wright, at Lewin's-Mead, Bristol, May 31, 1759* [1759].

Chaucer, Geoffrey. "Prologue to *The Canterbury Tales.*" In *The English Parnassus: An Anthology chiefly of Longer Poems,* edited by W. M. Dixon and H. J. C. Grierson, 1–18. Oxford: Clarendon, 1952.

Cocks, H. F. Lovell. "The Place of the Sermon in Worship." *The Expository Times* 49 (1938) 264–68.

Coggan, W. J. "The Minister as Pastor." In *The Congregational Ministry in the Modern World,* edited by H. Cunliffe-Jones, 105–16. London: Independent, 1955.

Cowper, William. "Mr. Village to Mr. Town." *The Connoisseur* 134 (19 August 1756). In *The British Essayists,* XXVI, edited by A. Chalmers, 358–63. London: n.p., 1823.

————. "The Task." London: Nisbet, 1855.

Cradock, Walter. *Glad Tydings from Heaven to the Worst of Sinners on Earth.* London: Mathew Simmons, 1648.

Creighton, Louise. *Life and Letters of Mandell Creighton.* 2 vols. London: Longmans, 1904.

Cunliffe-Jones, Hubert, ed. *The Congregational Ministry in the Modern World.* London: Independent, 1955.

Dart, John. "Stressed Out." *Christian Century,* 29 November 2003, 8–9.

Davies, J. Trevor. "The Minister as Preacher and Teacher." In *The Congregational Ministry in the Modern World,* edited by H. Cunliffe-Jones, 117–28. London: Independent, 1955.

Denney, James. *The Epistles to the Thessalonians.* London: Hodder and Stoughton, 1892.

————. *The Second Epistle to the Corinthians.* London: Hodder and Stoughton, 1916.

Densham, W., and J. Ogle. *The Story of the Congregational Churches of Dorset.* Bridport, UK: Mate, 1899.

de Quincey, Thomas. *Confessions of an English Opium Eater.* 1856. London: Bell, 1896.

Dods, Marcus (son), ed. *Early Letters of Marcus Dods.* London: Hodder and Stoughton, 1910.

Duncan, John. *Pulpit and Communion Table.* Edited by David Brown. Inverness, UK: Free Presbyterian, 1969.

Eachard, John. *The Grounds and Occasions of the Contempt of the Clergy and Religion Enquired into.* London: T. Davies, 1672.

Erasmus, D. *Ecclesiastes, or The Preacher.* London: Rivington, Faulder & Gardner, 1797.

Fairbairn, A. M., "Experience in Theology: A Chapter of Autobiography." *The Contemporary Review* 91 (January-June 1907) 554–73.

Figures, Joseph A. "The Value of a Liberal Education." In *The Congregational Ministry in the Modern World,* edited by H. Cunliffe-Jones, 27–37. London: Independent, 1955.

Flavel, John. *Works.* 6 vols. London: Banner of Truth, 1968.

Forsyth, P. T. *The Church and the Sacraments.* 1917. Reprint. London: Independent, 1964.

———. *The Church, the Gospel and Society.* London: Independent, 1962.

———. *Positive Preaching and the Modern Mind.* 1907. Reprint. London: Independent, 1949.

———. *The Principle of Authority.* 1913. Reprint. London: Independent, 1952.

———. *Revelation Old and New.* London: Independent, 1962.

Frost, J. "The Expediency of a Seminary in which Only an English Theological Education Should be Given." In *Minutes of the Proceedings of a Conference of Delegates, from the Committees of Various Theological Colleges connected with the Independent Churches of England and Wales,* 22–23. London: Blackburn and Pardon, 1845.

Goldsmith, Oliver. "The Deserted Village." In *The English Parnassus: An Anthology chiefly of Longer Poems,* edited by W. N. Dixon and H. J. C. Grierson, 225–33. Oxford: Clarendon Press, 1952.

Grant, James. *The Metropolitan Pulpit, or Sketches of the Most Popular Preachers in London.* London: George Virtue, 1839.

Grieve, Alexander J. "Christian Learning and Christian Living." In *The Congregational Year Book, 1937,* 70–83. London: Memorial Hall, 1937.

———. "A Hundred Years of Ministerial Training." *Transactions of the Congregational Historical Society* 11 (1932) 258–64.

Grove, Henry. *Ethical and Theological Writings.* 4 vols. 1747. Reprint. Bristol, UK: Thoemmes, 2000.

Hamilton, R. W. "On the Importance of drawing into the Ministry pious and devoted Young Men, from our more Educated and Wealthy Families." In *Minutes of the Proceedings of a Conference of Delegates from the Committees of Various Theological Colleges connected with the Independent Churches of England and Wales,* 25–31. London: Blackburn and Pardon, 1845.

Harman, Allan. "The Place of the Biblical Languages in the Theological Curriculum." *Reformed Theological Review* 50 (1991) 91–97.

Haslam, William. *From Life to Death.* London: Jarrold, 1894.

Henry, Matthew. *The Life of the Rev. Philip Henry, A.M.* 1698. Reprint. Edinburgh: Banner of Truth, 1974.

Horsch, John. *Modern Religious Liberalism.* Chicago: The Bible Institute Colportage Association, 1920.

Houlden, Leslie. "Education in Theology: Story and Prospects." *Theology* 111 (2008) 170–77.

Hull, J. H. Eric. *The Holy Spirit in the Acts of the Apostles.* London: Lutterworth, 1967.

Huxtable, W. John F. "Thoughts on Ministerial Training." *The Congregational Quarterly* 33 (1955) 141–50.

Illingworth, J. R. *University and Cathedral Sermons.* London: Macmillan, 1893.

Jay, William. *Autobiography.* Edited by George Redfors and John Angell James. 1854. Reprint. Edinburgh: Banner of Truth, 1974.

Jenkins, Daniel T. *The Gift of Ministry.* London: Faber and Faber, 1947.

———. *The Protestant Ministry.* London: Faber and Faber, 1958.

John, Glynmor. *Congregationalism in an Ecumenical Era.* London: Independent, 1967.

Johnson, Anthony B. Review of *Leading God's People: Wisdom from the Early Church for Today,* by Christopher A. Beeley. Grand Rapids: Eerdmans, 2012. *The Christian Century,* 7 August 2013, 40.

Kennedy, John. *The Days of the Fathers in Ross-shire*. 2nd ed. Edinburgh: John Maclaren, 1861.

Kirk, E. N. *The Obligations of the Church to Secure a Learned and Pious Ministry. Preached at the Anniversary of Cheshunt College, July 4th, 1839*. London: John Snow, 1839.

Knox, John. *The History of the Reformation in Scotland*. London: Melrose, 1905.

Leckie, J. H. *David W. Forrest, DD*. London: Hodder and Stoughton, 1919.

Lockley, G. Lindsay. *Early Congregationalism in Queensland*. Edited by John Wheeler. Brisbane: Queensland Congregational Fellowship, 2004.

Luke, W. B. *Memorials of F. W. Bourne*. London: W. H. Gregory, 1906.

Mackennal, Alexander. *Life of John Allison Macfadyen*. London: Hodder and Stoughton, 1891.

Mackenzie, Robert. *John Brown of Haddington*. 1918. Reprint. London: Banner of Truth, 1964.

McLachlan, Herbert. *Essays and Addresses*. Manchester: Manchester University Press, 1950.

Manning, Bernard Lord. *A Layman in the Ministry*. London: Independent, 1942.

Manson, T. W. *The Church's Ministry*. London: Hodder and Stoughton, 1948.

———. *Ministry and Priesthood: Christ's and Ours*. London: Epworth, 1958.

Miall, J. G. *Congregationalism in Yorkshire*. London: Snow, 1868.

Milton, John. "Lycidas." In *Collected English Verse: An Anthology chosen by Margaret and Ronald Bottrall*, 206–12. London: Sidgwick and Jackson, 1946.

Moody-Stuart, Kenneth. *Brownlow North: His Life and Work*. 1878. Reprint. London: Banner of Truth, 1961.

Neil, William. *The Plain Man Looks at the Bible*. London: Collins, 1956.

Newton, John. *Memoirs of the Life of the Late William Grimshaw*. London: Religious Tract Society, 1832.

Orton, Job. *Letters to Dissenting Ministers*. Edited by S. Palmer. 2 vols. London: Longman, Hurst, Rees and Orme, 1806.

Owen, John. *Works*. Edited by William H. Goold. 1850–53. Reprint. London: Banner of Truth, 1967.

Paul, Robert S. *Ministry*. Grand Rapids: Eerdmans, 1965.

Peel, Albert. *These Hundred Years: A History of the Congregational Union of England and Wales, 1831–1931*. London: The Congregational Union, 1931.

Peel, Albert, and J. A. R. Marriott. *Robert Forman Horton*. London: Allen & Unwin, 1937.

Peel, David R. *Ministry for Mission*. Manchester: Northern College, 2003.

———. *The Story of the Moderators*. London: The United Reformed Church, 2012.

Plowright, B. C. "The Holy Spirit in the Work of the Ministry." In *The Congregational Ministry in the Modern World*, edited by H. Cunliffe-Jones, 141–53. London: Independent, 1955.

Poole-Connor, E. J. *Evangelicalism in England*. Worthing, UK: Walter, 1965.

Porritt, Arthur. *John Henry Jowett, CH, MA, DD*. London: Hodder and Stoughton, 1924.

Powicke, F. J. *David Worthington Simon*. London: Hodder and Stoughton, 1912.

Pratt, A. C. *Black Country Methodism*. London: Charles H. Kelly, 1891.

Ragsdale, William Oates. *They Sought a Land: A Settlement in the Arkansas River Valley 1840–1870*. Fayetteville, AR: University of Arkansas Press, 1997.

Reindorp, George. *Putting It Over: Ten Points for Preachers*. London: Hodder and Stoughton, 1961.

Reynolds, H. R. *Notes on the Christian Life: A Selection of Sermons*. London: Macmillan, 1865.

———. "On the formation of a Federal Board, empowered to grant Degrees in Theology to successful Competitors for such Honours." In *Minutes of the Proceedings of a Conference of Delegates from the Committees of Various Theological Colleges connected with the Independent Churches of England and Wales*, 41–50. London: Jackson, 1865.

Robinson, John. *Works*. 3 vols. London: John Snow, 1851.

[Robinson, W. Gordon]. *Our Heritage of Free Prayer*. London: Congregational Union of England and Wales, n.d.

Rogers, Henry. *Essays, Selected from Contributions to The Edinburgh Review*. 3 vols. London: Long, Brown, Green, and Longmans, 1850–55.

Romaine, William. *Letters from the late Rev. William Romaine, M.A., . . . to a Friend*. Oxford: Thomas Wills, 1809.

Roth, Jeffrey. "Who Will Serve?" *The Mercersburg Practitioner* 4 (Spring 2002) 2–4.

Ryle, J. C. *Five Christian Leaders of the Eighteenth Century*. London: Banner of Truth, 1960.

Scott, John. *Life of the Rev. Thomas Scott, D.D.* London: L. B. Seeley, 1822.

Sell, Alan P. F. *Aspects of Christian Integrity*. 1990. Reprint. Eugene, OR: Wipf & Stock, 1998.

———. *Commemorations: Studies in Christian Thought and History*. 1993. Reprint. Eugene, OR: Wipf & Stock, 1998.

———. *Confessing the Faith Yesterday and Today: Essays Reformed, Dissenting, and Catholic*. Eugene, OR: Pickwick, 2013.

———. *Dissenting Thought and the Life of the Churches: Studies in an English Tradition*. Lewiston, NY: Mellen, 1990.

———. *Doctrine and Devotion*. Vol. 1: *God Our Father*; Vol. 2: *Christ Our Saviour*; Vol. 3: *The Spirit Our Life*. Shippensburg, PA: Ragged Edge, 2000.

———. *Enlightenment, Ecumenism, Evangel: Theological Themes and Thinkers 1550–2000*. Milton Keynes, UK: Paternoster, 2005.

———. *Guidelines on Church Discipline*. London: The United Reformed Church, 1983.

———. *Nonconformist Theology in the Twentieth Century*. Didsbury Lectures. Milton Keynes, UK: Paternoster, 2006.

———. *Philosophy, Dissent and Nonconformity, 1689–1920*. 2004. Reprint. Eugene, OR: Wipf & Stock, 2009.

———. *Philosophy, History and Theology: Selected Reviews, 1975–2011*. Eugene, OR: Wipf & Stock, 2012.

———. *Saints: Visible, Orderly, and Catholic: The Congregational Idea of the Church*. Eugene, OR: Pickwick, 1986.

———. *Testimony and Tradition: Studies in Reformed and Dissenting Thought*. 2005. Reprint. Eugene, OR: Wipf & Stock, 2012.

———. *The Theological Education of the Ministry: Soundings in the British Reformed and Dissenting Traditions*. Eugene, OR: Pickwick, 2013.

———. "The Unsung Ministers of Congregationalism's List B." *The Journal of The United Reformed Church History Society*, forthcoming.

Shakespeare, William. *The Tempest*. In *The Complete Works of William Shakespeare*, edited by Charles Jasper Sisson. London: Odhams, 1953.

Sibbes, Richard. *Works*. 1862–64. Reprint. Edinburgh: Banner of Truth, 1973.

Simon, D. W. "The Congregational Ministry in the British Isles." *The British Weekly,* 17 January 1901, 374.

———. "Theological Training for Ministerial Students." In *Memorial of the Opening of the New and Enlarged Buildings of Lancashire Independent College,* 78–92. Manchester: Tubbs and Brook, 1879.

Simpson, P. Carnegie. "The Character of Presbytery." *The Congregational Quarterly* 23 (October 1945) 306–16.

Slate, R. *A Brief History of the Rise and Progress of the Lancashire Congregational Union; and of the Blackburn Independent Academy.* London: Hamilton Adams, 1840.

Spurgeon, C. H. *An All-Round Ministry: Addresses to Ministers and Students.* 1900. Reprint. London: Banner of Truth, 1960.

Stackhouse, Max L. "Contextualization and Theological Education." *ATS Theological Education* 23 (Autumn 1986) 67–84.

Stanyon, Nick. Letter to *Reform* (October 2003) 25.

Stoughton, John. *Reminiscences of Congregationalism Fifty Years Ago.* London: Hodder and Stoughton, 1881.

Stowell, W. Hendry. *An Address to the Students of Cheshunt College . . . on his Public Recognition as President.* London: Snow, 1850.

Taylor, John. *The Scripture Account of Prayer.* London: n.p., 1762.

Thompson, David M. *Let Sects and Parties Fall: A Short History of the Association of Churches of Christ in Great Britain and Ireland.* Birmingham: Berean,1980.

———, ed. *Stating the Gospel: Formulations and Declarations of Faith from the Heritage of The United Reformed Church.* Edinburgh: T. & T. Clark, 1990.

Torrance, Iain R. "Thomas F. Torrance's Theology of Ministry and the Pressing Issues of Today." *The Expository Times* 124 (August 2013) 521–29.

Torrance, T. F. *Conflict and Agreement in the Church.* 2 vols. 1960. Reprint. Eugene, OR: Wipf & Stock, 1996.

Tucker, Tony. *Reformed Ministry: Traditions of Ministry and Ordination in The United Reformed Church.* London: The United Reformed Church, 2003.

Vaughan, Robert. *Protestant Nonconformity in Its Relation to Learning and Piety. An Inaugural Discourse delivered at the opening of the Lancashire Independent College.* London: n.p., 1843.

Wadsworth, Kenneth W. "Open to the World." *Reform* (May 1990) 12.

Watson, Thomas. *A Body of Divinity.* 1692. Reprint. London: Banner of Truth, 1965.

———. *A Divine Cordial.* 1663. Reprint. Grand Rapids: Sovereign Grace, 1971.

Watts, Isaac. *A Guide to Prayer.* 1715. Abridged and edited by Harry Escott. London: Epworth, 1948.

Williams, J. B. *Memoirs of the Life, Character, and Writings of the Rev. Matthew Henry.* 1828. Reprint. Edinburgh: Banner of Truth, 1972.

Withers, John. *A Charge given to Mr. Micaijah Towgood, at his Ordination in Moreton Hampstead, Devon, August 21, 1722* [1723].

# Descriptive Index of Persons

This index comprises the names of, and gives an indication of the work done by, deceased ministers who served The United Reformed Church and its predecessor traditions. The following abbreviations are used:

C:      Congregational
CC:     Churches of Christ
CCEW:   Congregational Church in England and Wales
CUEW:   Congregational Union of England and Wales
ICC:    International Congregational Council
LMS:    London Missionary Society
P:      Presbyterian
PCE:    Presbyterian Church of England
UR:     United Reformed
URC:    United Reformed Church
WCC:    World Council of Churches

Adeney, Walter Frederic (1849–1920) [C], Professor, New College, London; President, Lancashire Independent College, Manchester, 94

Alexander, William Lindsay (1808–84) [C], Principal Congregational Theological Hall, Edinburgh, 85

Alliott, Richard (1804–63) [C], President, Western College, Plymouth; Cheshunt College; Professor, Spring Hill College, Birmingham, 85

Amory, Thomas (1700/01–74) [P], Taunton Academy; Old Jewry, London, 24, 81

Ashworth, Caleb (1722–75) [C], Daventry Academy, 82

Bagshawe, William (1628–1702) [P], "apostle of the Peak" (Derbyshire), 49–50, 68

Barnes, Thomas (1747–1810) [P], Cross Street, Manchester; Manchester Academy, 82

Bennett, William Henry (1855–1920) [C], Professor, Rotherham, Hackney and New Colleges; Principal, Lancashire Independent College, Manchester, 94–95

Grove, Henry (1683–1738), [P],
Taunton Academy, 24, 81

Hall, [Christopher John] Newman
(1816–1902), [C], Surrey Chapel,
London, 10

Hamilton, Richard Winter (1794–
1848), [C], Albion/Belgrave, Leeds,
14, 15n28

Hart, Joseph (1722–68] [C], Jewin
Street, London; hymn writer, 29

Henry, Matthew (1662–1714), [P],
Chester; Bible commentator, 58,
63n57

Henry, Philip (1631–96), [P], ejected
1662; Dodington, Whitchurch,
Salop; tutor, Broad Oak, Flint, 62–63

Hill, Rowland (1744–1833), [C], Surrey Chapel, London, 53–54, 77

Hodgson, James Muscutt (1841–1923),
[C], Professor, Lancashire Independent College; Principal, Congregational Theological Hall, Edinburgh,
85

Horton, Robert Forman (1855–1934),
[C], Lyndhurst Road, Hampstead,
London, 41

Howe, John (1630–1705), [P], ejected
1662; Haberdashers' Hall, London;
author, 64

Hughes, Thomas Hywel (1875–1945),
[C], Principal, Scottish Congregational College, 85

Hull, [John Howarth] Eric (1923–77),
[C/UR], Professor then Principal,
Northern Congregational College.
Manchester, 100n48

Huxtable, [William] John [Fairchild]
(1912–90), Principal, New College,
London; Secretary, CUEW, CCEW,
URC; Secretary, Churches Unity
Commission, 105

James, [William] Andrew (1904–
1975), [C/UR], Moderator, Southern
Province, CUEW, 100n46

Jay, William (1769–1863), [C], Argyle,
Bath, 1, 2n5

Jenkins, Daniel Thomas (1914–2002),
[C/UR], ecumenist and theologian,
55, 60

John, Glynmor (1903–92), [C], Sutton;
ICC, 8n10

Jones, Samuel (1628–97), [P], Brynllywarch Academy, Glamorgan, 84

Jowett, John Henry (1863–1923),
[C], Westminster Chapel; eminent
preacher, 32

King, David (1819–94), [CC], evangelist and pioneer educator of men for
"Gospel work," 86

Leatherland, Harold Fulton (1909–77),
[C], Headingly Hill, Leeds; thence to
Australia; liturgiologist, 34n13

Lewis, Howel Elfed (Elvet) (1860–
1953), [C], King's Cross, London;
poet and hymn writer, 29

M'Cartney, John (d. 1949, *aet.* 95)
[CC], correspondence tutor;
lecturer, Overdale College, Birmingham, 86

Macfadyen, John Allison (1837–99),
[C], Chorlton Road, Manchester,
66–67

Mackennal, Alexander (1835–1904),
[C], Bowdon, Cheshire; Secretary,
ICC; author, 67n72

Mackintosh, Robert (1858–1933), [C],
Professor, Lancashire Independent
College, Manchester, 94, 95

Manson, Thomas Walter (1893–1958),
[P], John Rylands Professor of
Biblical Criticism and Exegesis,
University of Manchester, 4, 6

Marsh, John (1904–94), [C/UR], first
Professor of Theology, University of
Nottingham; Principal, Mansfield
College, Oxford, 85

Miall, James Goodeve (1805–96), [C],
Salem, Bradford; historian of Yorkshire Congregationalism, 21n45

# General Index

*Note*: While Congregational and Presbyterian institutions are listed in this index, the lone terms "Congregational" and "Presbyterian" are not, for they are ubiquitous in the main text.